Reasons for the name, "30 Seconds."

Jimmy Parker's legendary genealogy filing system. Jimmy Parker is the former Manager, Main Library Operations, Genealogy Library in Salt Lake City. Over the last twenty years he has been a popular teacher and lecturer. His classrooms have been well attended. On many occasions, he has discussed the principles of the organization of papers and documents. He is passionate about an organized filing system. He has always said that, *"You need to organize a filing system that will allow you to find a document within thirty (30) seconds."* Jimmy has organized his genealogy files so that he can find all of his documents and papers. He has practiced what he taught.

FIRST EDITION

Publisher:
Heritage Knights, LLC
84 West 7500 South
Midvale, Utah 84047

Web page: www.needhelpto .com

ISBN # 0-9712526-0-2

Table of Contents

Acknowledgments

This book was written because a need developed. The need is for many genealogy researchers to organize their papers. This book was written because of a desire to assist others in doing a better job with their genealogy. It all started with a few ideas and a filing system resulted. It started with the help of friends and associates, who expressed interest, encouragement and confidence in this project.

Wayne Morris, Regional Manager of Field Acquisitions, Genealogical Society of Utah, and Bob Langman have been friends for twenty years. Bob has a facility for organization. He taught classes at the University in Business Organizational Behavior. Wayne and Bob have talked many times about genealogy and organizing their files. About seven years ago, they developed an organizational concept that worked. They began to use the system and perfected it. Wayne suggested that a book needed to be written.

Wayne introduced Bob to Jimmy Parker. Jimmy is an author, past manager of the Genealogy Library in Salt Lake City, Utah, and a highly respected genealogist. Bob kept an appointment with Jimmy Parker to introduce his concept of organizing and filing papers and documents in a genealogy filing system. Jimmy agreed with the concept because his organizational system was similar. After much thought, discussion and work, it was decided to publish the book, "30 Seconds," A Guide to Organizing Your Genealogy Files.

The authors are so very grateful to their beloved wives, Sherry Parker and Sharon Langman, for their support and encouragement. Their support was essential for the completion of this book.

Foreword

This book is written for you.

This book is written for the beginning genealogist who wants to pursue this hobby and is committed to learning and doing. This is for the beginner who wants to be organized and prepared.

This book is written for the tens of millions of genealogists who have done some research and experienced the joy of this "hands on" hobby. They have taken a class or two and have learned to do their genealogy research. They are learning on their own by talking to more experienced researchers and doing their own work. As they collect documents and information they put these papers into piles. The piles grow and there is nowhere to put them.

This book is written for the experienced genealogist who needs to learn a few principles of organization and thus better organize their papers so that they know where to put them and then find those documents in their files.

This book is written for the many executives and professionals who find it hard to do their own research so they hire a genealogy researcher. When they receive their notebook of research information, they need an organized filing system in which to put their papers. They need to pull the research notebook apart and put the papers into an organized filing system or cross-reference their file to the notebook so they can find any document within "30 seconds."

Prologue

"This is how I lost heart in doing my genealogy work"

I started my genealogy research about twenty years ago. I learned how to research by taking classes in genealogy. I learned as much as I could and began to do the research. I met with my grandmother who knew all about the family. She was anxious to help. I made copies of a lot of her documents and papers. She gave me pictures and explained in detail who was in the picture, where it was taken and who took the picture.

With this knowledge and grandma's information, I began to research with great enthusiasm. I found birth certificates, baptism records, marriage certificates, census records, land records and probate records, I enjoyed every minute.

I collected all these pictures, papers and documents and put them into piles by surname. I had several piles all over my office at home. Each pile included parents, grandparents, great grandparents and other relatives. The folders were thick with papers but disorganized, although everything was there. I then found a box and some manila folders. I put a pile of papers by surname into the manila folders, I put the surname on the manila folder tab. I put the pile into the file. Then I put the "file with the pile" into the box for safekeeping. When I finished I had four boxes of valuable papers and I felt safe.

On several occasions I went to the library to do research in the 1880 census. I soon realized I had seen the census entry for this family before. I was repeating my research efforts. I was lost. I didn't know where I was or where I was going. I felt like I was going in circles. I needed to do something.

My cousin, Joyce, called and asked for Aunt Lanna's birth certificate. I was happy to accommodate but couldn't find it. I had forgotten that I had moved one of the boxes downstairs. I became embarrassed and discouraged about my genealogy. I was a good researcher but couldn't find many of my documents and repeated my efforts. I was losing heart for genealogy. I needed to do something.

I found published information with my surnames. Other researchers had completed good research on the surnames but had not proven my names were related. I hadn't proven the links. Because I was disorganized, I allowed myself to think that further research was not necessary. I began to think that these ties were related to mine.

Then, something interesting happened. As I became confused and disoriented in my research work, I concluded that there was nothing left for me to do. So I began to think that I must have completed my research, if I didn't know what to do next, I must be finished. I needed to do something and soon.

This is a common story among those interested in family and genealogy. There is a solution and it is simple. The solution is to organize your papers and documents into a logical filing system. When you organize, your heart will be warmed. Organize your genealogy and this important work will reach great heights.

Robert Langman

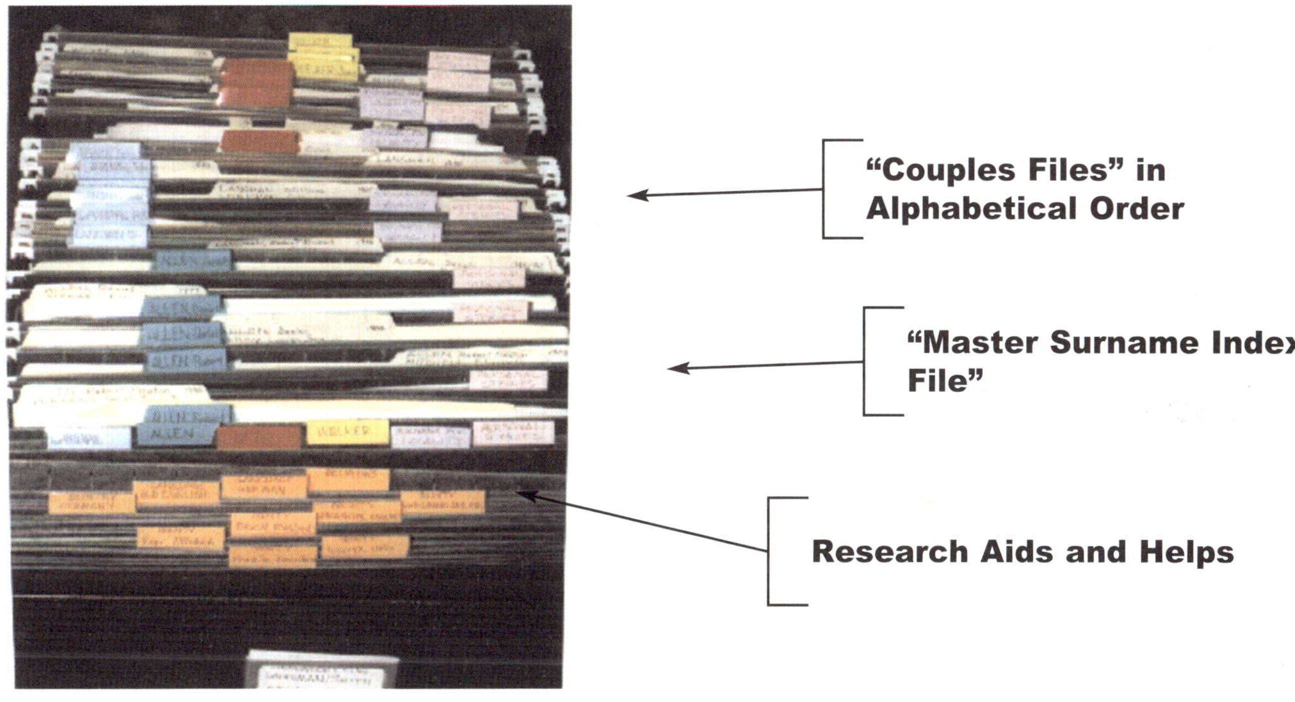

Couples' Files organized by Surname, (Blue)Langman, (Green)Allen, (Red)Smith, (Yellow)Walker, (Orange) Aids, and Helps, (Purple) Surname by Locality, (Pink) Personal Stories.

Chapter 1 When you Organize, Success Will Follow

There is a good reason for having an organized genealogy filing system The purpose of a filing system is to put a document away and then quickly be able to find it at a later time. The goal is to organize your papers in such a way that will allow you to find a document successfully. When you are able to find your papers, you succeed.

When you put your papers in a file with no organization, you will probably be unsuccessful in finding them. Then the frustration begins. After a time of frustration, you will lose interest in doing genealogy work. There are many inactive genealogy researchers out there who have lost heart in their genealogy, simply because they were unorganized. Does this statement sound familiar?

> *"I spent years collecting documents and papers, most of the papers went into my files; other papers went into boxes that later ended up downstairs. When I wanted a specific document I couldn't find it. I spent too much time looking for my papers. After awhile I lost interest in my genealogy, and for the next few years I would talk about it but did little."*

When you organize your files properly in a neat and orderly manner, you avoid confusion and inactivity. Confusion breeds inactivity.

> *"We all know of many genealogy researchers who spend a lot of time talking about their genealogy research, but have lost heart."*

"One colour, indeed, they say the chameleon cannot assume; it cannot itself appear white." *-Plutarch, Alcibiades, page 249.*

The chameleon can change itself into any color but white. Everyone has his or her own talents and limitations. It is no secret that everyone has his or her own way of doing genealogy research. Learn the organization concepts; then make a system that fits your personality! You make your own system.

Order is the first step toward mastering your genealogy. Order and organization brings success and completion to the work. You know where you are in your research and what you need to do next. You have order in all things around you.

When you are able to find your papers, You are a success. When you put your papers away so that anyone can find them, you are a success.

What do I do with all this research?

Genealogy is the work of family relationships. It takes a lot of work and cooperation to accumulate information. Your files should be preserved and passed down to the next generation, so that others will benefit from your work. Knowing your family history and facts about your ancestors brings family unity. Genealogy work should go on from one generation to the next. Someone once said that, "there is one important gift we can give our children and that is our "roots." Passing on this work is important because it ties the family together.

> *"Nancy, my daughter knew she wanted to do genealogy when she was 16 years old. In the next few years, she will be ready to accept the responsibility for the genealogy work. She is now 19 years old attending Southern Utah University. She is on scholarship playing women's basketball, dating boys and studying to be a Pediatrician. I am putting my genealogy in order so when she is ready, I can present her my organized work with good conscience."*
>
> -**Robert Langman**

When you pass on your genealogy work it would be nice to give your successor a genealogy that is organized. Get organized and prepare your Family history in a neat and orderly manner. Whoever succeeds you will be eternally grateful and the gift of your "roots" will be more valuable.

The Computer and Printer Will be Used to Create Genealogy Documents

It is not necessary to use a computer in genealogy research but it is simpler and easier to use the computer and printer for this presentation. The data management program in the computer will be used to enter information and then print documents. The use of a computer management system program is like using pencil or typewriter to record your information. After the information is recorded the papers are filed away in a filing system.

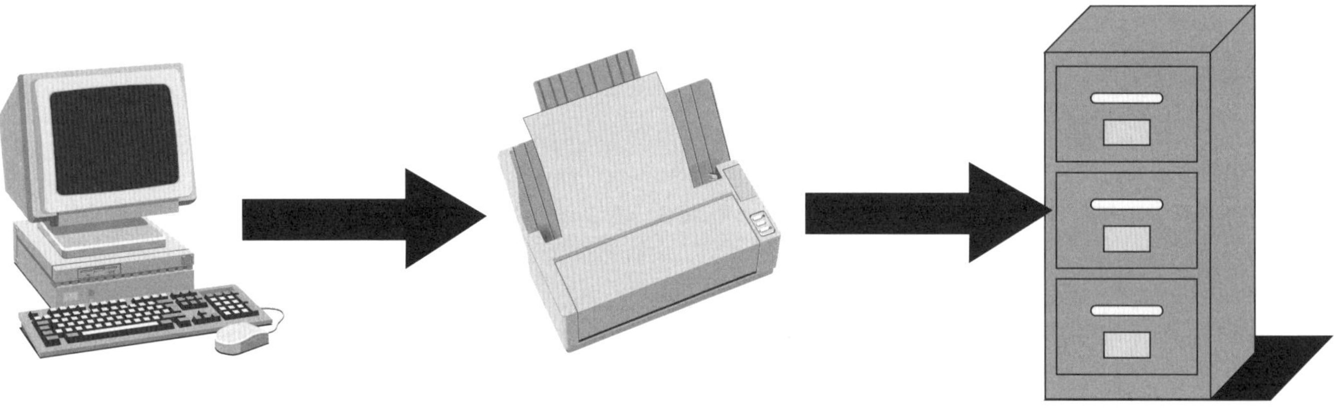

"No two people are alike and both like it that way." - Anonymous

People have their own way of doing things. Everyone does things differently. In genealogy there is more than one way to file materials so they can be found quickly and there is more than one way to do it effectively. It is our goal to explain a system that works.

The system here is one approach in filing. Many prefer a straight alphabetical filing sequence, others prefer a numbering system. How you do it is a personal preference. It is hoped that you, the reader will adapt some of these principles and ideas into a system of your liking.

It is possible to have a predictable and well-organized filing system. This is a system of order. The first section of your filing system (orange) includes your research aids (like local city maps) and helps (like references on local churches or background history of a locality).

The second item to be discussed here is the "Master Surname Index File." This is a master guide showing the position and color of tabs of the four grandparents lines. The "Master Surname Index File" is a hanging file folder with five or six-tab positions. The legal has six positions and the letter sized has five-tab positions (shown in the photograph). The position of the SURNAME tab will identify your four grand parents ancestral lines (The four tabs colors are blue, green, red and yellow). The "Master Surname Index File" is a guide of color and position showing your four grandparents ancestral lines.

The third section is the part of the file, which contains detailed information about each couple and their children. It is called the "Couples File." It contains information already known about the couple and suggestions for what needs to be done next to further identify them.

If you follow these principles, your filing system will be neat, organized, and orderly.

This is what your filing system should look when it is finished!

Couples' files in alphabetical order

"Master SURNAME Index File"

Research Aids and Helps (orange)

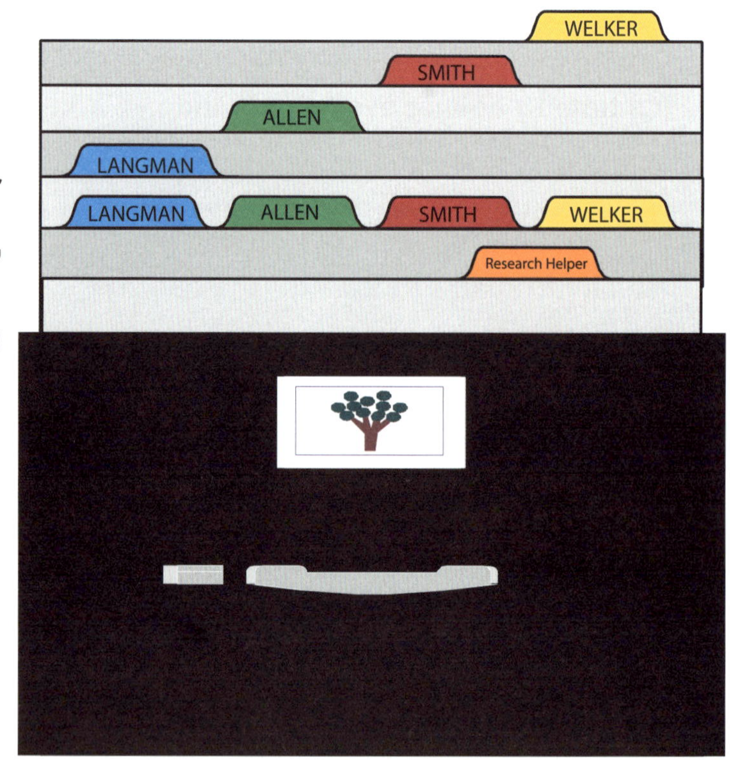

"The beginning is the most important part of the work." *Plato, c. 428-349*

Let's begin the work! We need to be smart as we start. Sometimes it takes courage to start anew. We will go one step at a time until your genealogy filing system becomes organized.

Chapter 2 Getting Started With Yours

Review from Chapter 1

1. The filing system presented here is an example of a system that works very well.
2. Learn organizational principles and techniques.
3. Develop a filing system that fits your personality and works for you.

It's time to collect everything and put it into one place:

Collect all your genealogy materials. To make this easy, select a place in your home as a workspace for your genealogy. You will need at least a table or desk and a chair. A legal or letter size filing cabinet would be very helpful. The legal size file drawer is important if you are in preserving many old documents.

Many of the older documents were written on legal size paper, so rather than fold the legal document it is better to keep the paper unfolded in the file. A letter size file cabinet may also be used. If a file cabinet is not available, then a cardboard or strong plastic file box may be used.

Step 1:

Put papers and documents into one place

"My wife makes a detailed shopping list. She tells me what is on the list and to listen carefully. When I get to the grocery store, I often forget the list and buy the groceries from memory. That is usually a mistake."

You may need to have these items available; if you don't, then buy the following items:

In order to set up a well organized genealogy file system it is necessary to have a few supplies. You may already have some of these items. If not make the following items available for use.

Take this list with you and use it to buy any missing items.

Required:

- Note pad 81/2 X 11, acid free paper (to take notes for future reference)
- Black Ink pen, fine point (used to take notes for future reference)
- Pencils for recording information in archival settings
- Black Ink pen, medium point (used to print names and dates on manila folder tabs)
- Legal or letter size hanging file folders (to be put into filing cabinet)
- Vinyl tabs for hanging folders 1/5 cut (to be attached to hanging folders)
- Legal or letter size manila folders 1/3 cut (to be dropped into hanging file folder)
- Large pedigree chart (to be hung on wall for reference)
- Acid-free printer paper for pedigree charts and Family Groups Records

Prepare Forms to Help You Organize

Now, create the documents that will summarize what you know. From the papers and documents collected, record the information manually or on the data management program of your computer and print the following reports.

1- The pedigree chart of five generations (See illustration on page 65). The pedigree chart ties the direct line generations together, i.e. son to father, father to grandfather and so on. The pedigree chart is a table of contents of all your family group records

Step 2:

Create Family Group Records and Prepare Research Notes

2- Family group record (see illustration on pages 66 & 67) listing each set of parents with their children.

3- Research notes (See illustration on page 68 & 69). Research notes could be the most important documents in your file. They are a summary of all the research done in the past on each family group. They are summaries of present notations, as well as any future plans for research. Your notes should include all appropriate annotations and document sources, then be placed in the couples file next to the family group sheet.

Step 3:

Create Pedigree Charts

4- Documents: A primary document is written when an event takes place and is recorded from testimony of an eyewitness, such as a birth or marriage. A secondary document is recorded after an event, such as a published genealogy or other compilations of data.

Step 4:

Using the Hanging File Folder, make The Surname File

Examples of these documents are:
- Certificates and documents for birth, baptism, marriage, death, burial and any other event to be researched.
- Documents from the home, town, county, state, national sources already researched
- The research papers of others
- Photographs

It is important to know the status of your research. Any genealogy researcher should be able to go to into their notes and understand the current status of their research. If your notes are complete and well documented, you will be able to take the next step in research. Using this filing system will result in less duplication of work, fewer errors and less frustration.

Prepare these forms:

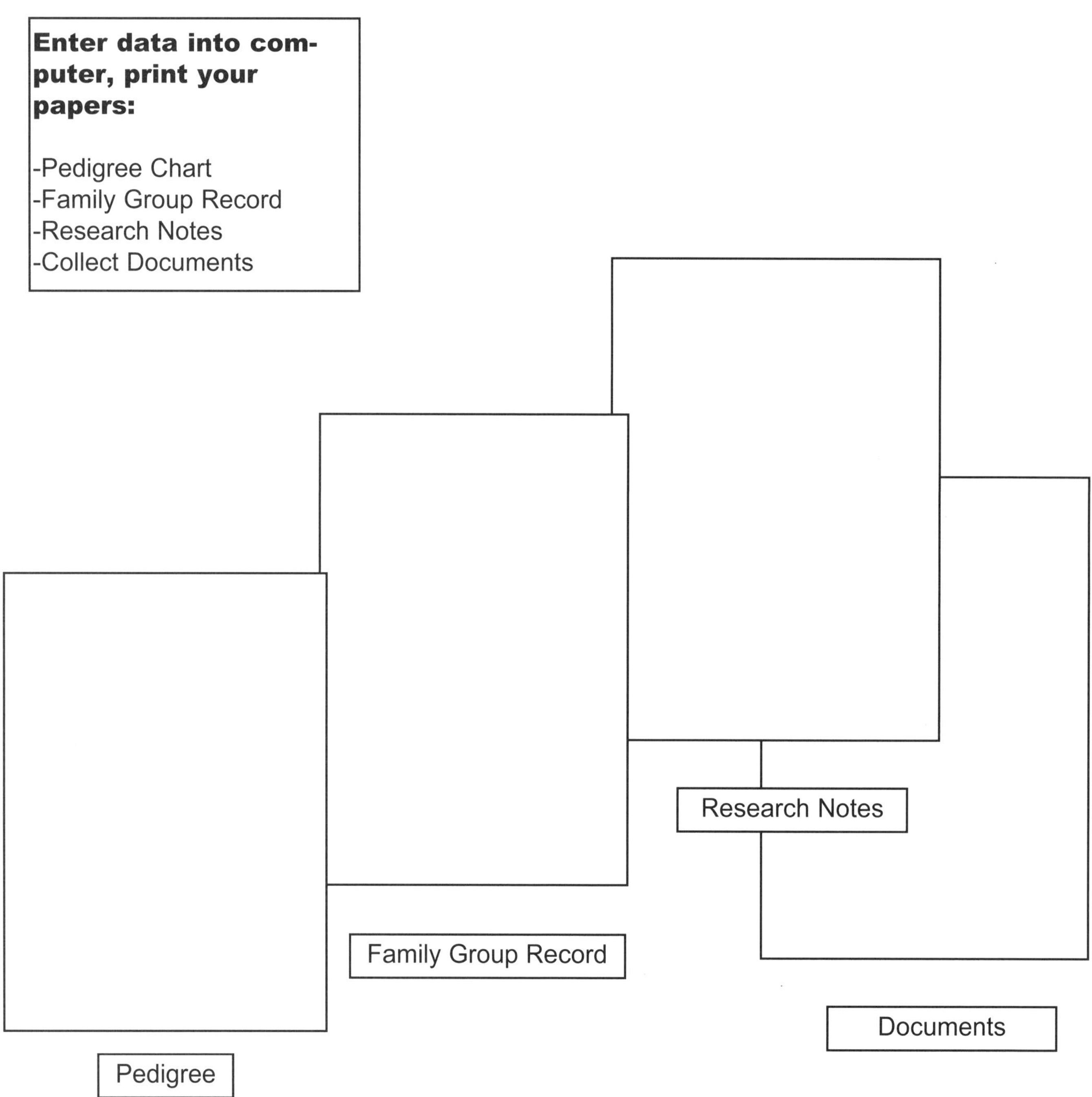

Family group records go into the files in alphabetical order:

"The simplest way is to file it in alphabetical order."

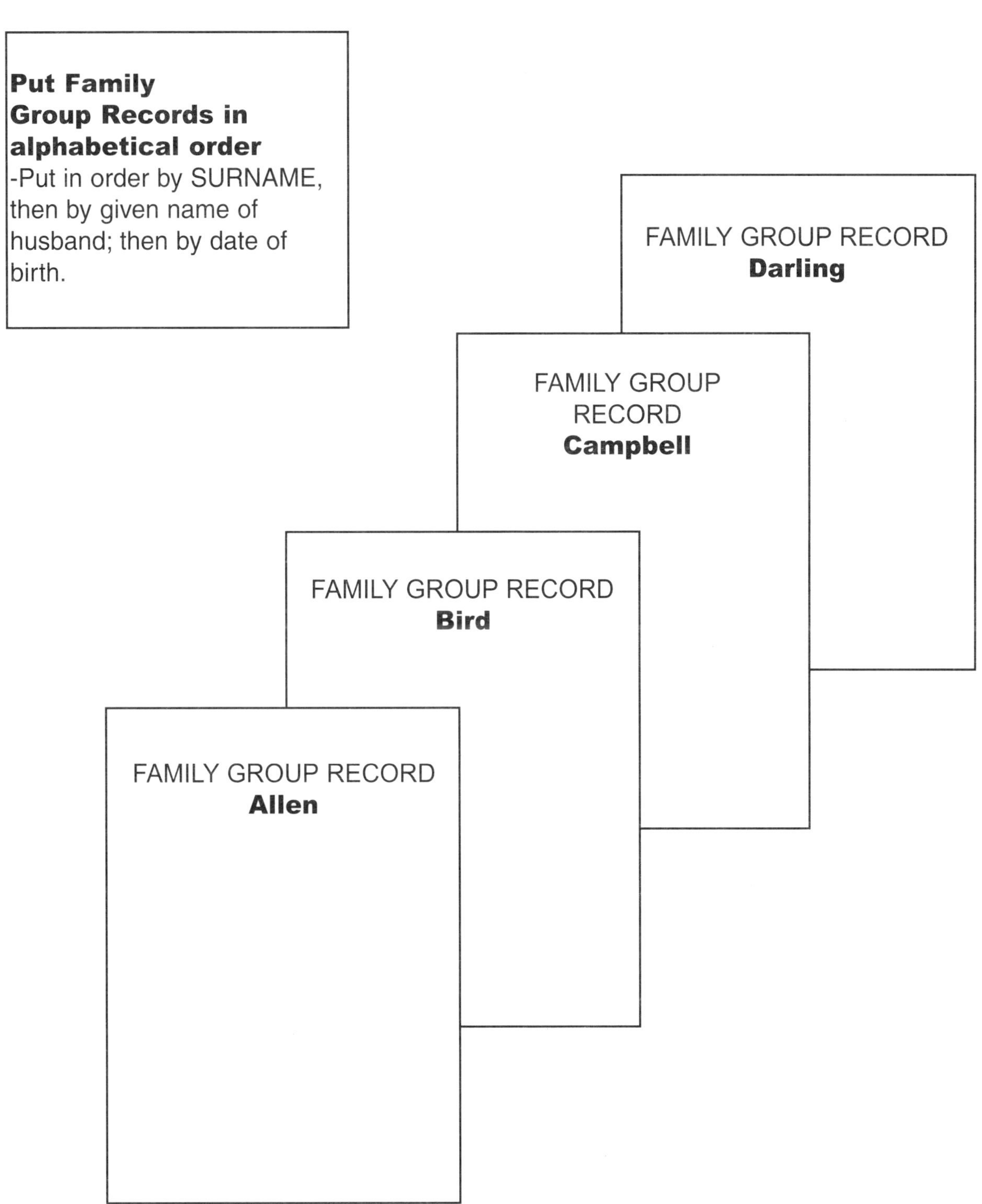

Now, Put Your Pedigree Charts into Your Files

Your pedigree chart should be the first paper you put into your file.

A Place for Your Pedigree Charts

-Put your pedigree chart in front of all your records. They show how your family groups are related.

After your data has been entered, make 16 copies of the five-generation pedigree chart; highlight the person under study on each of the sixteen names on the pedigree charts.

After you enter the data taken from the primary documents into the data management program, print 16 copies of the completed pedigree charts. Highlight your SURNAME and first name on your pedigree chart with a yellow highlighter. Then, on another chart highlight the father, then the grandfather and so forth. The goal is to put sixteen (16) Family Group Records and a highlighted pedigree chart into each couple's file folder.

Step 5:

On the hanging file folder, insert a vinyl tab with a printed SURNAME

Then, you will extend the sixteen names on the pedigree chart:

There should be a couple's file for every couple on the pedigree chart. As you extend your Pedigree charts to additional charts make an extended file. The extended numbers are 2 through 17.

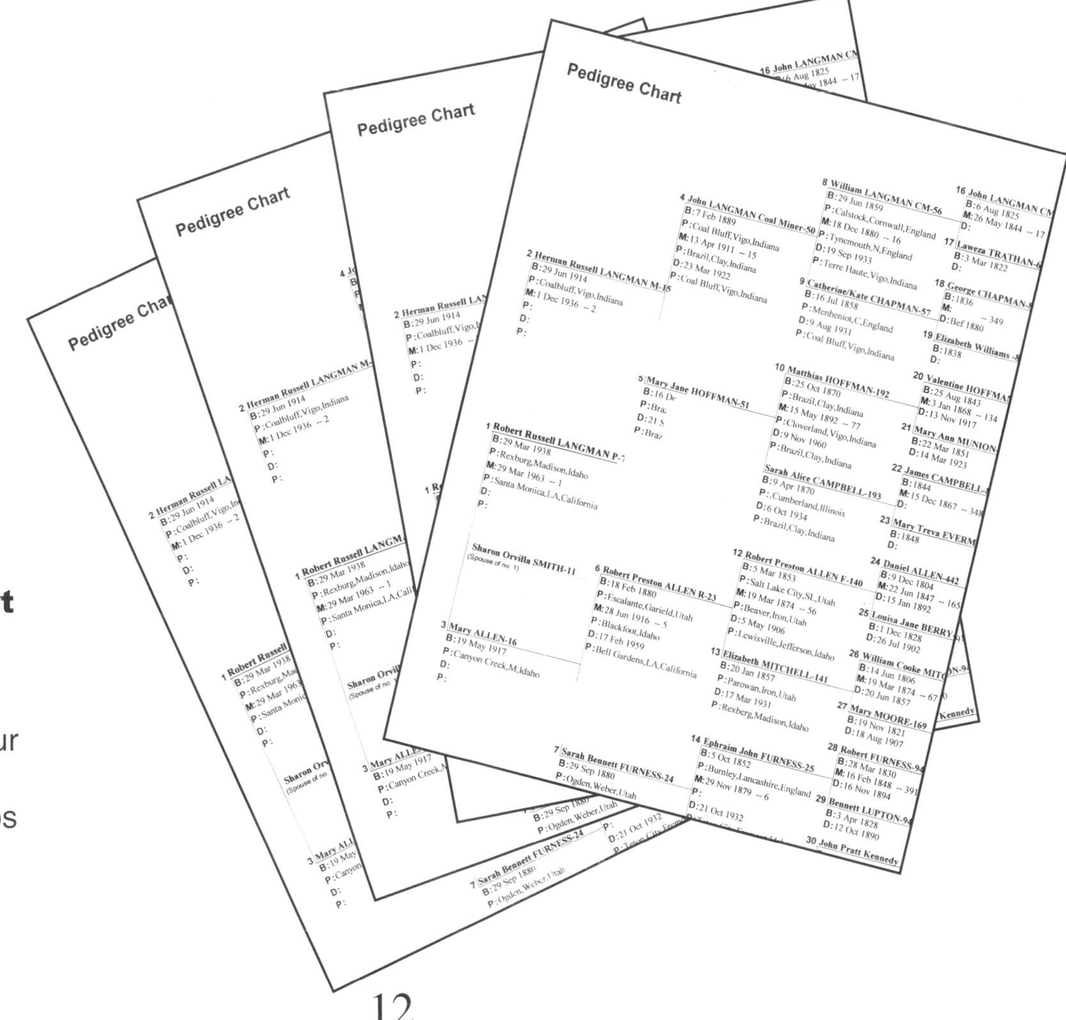

Five (5) Generation Chart -To extend the 5 generation chart

-Put your pedigree chart in front of all your records. They show how your family groups are related.

Chapter 3 "Organizing Your Couples' Files"

Review from Chapter 2

1. Collect everything and put it in one place...a box or filing cabinet.
2. Create pedigree charts
3. Create family group records
4. Prepare research notes
5. Collect documents

"Thou shouldest set in order the things that are wanting..." *Titus 1: 5*

The couples' file folder is a place to put the genealogy researcher's most important information. A couple's file includes the records of a husband and wife as a couple, along with their children. It contains all the documents looked for and found in your research effort. This file is a collection of all the documents and papers that prove who your ancestors are.

This file should also include a written summary of information not found or "negative searches." Always include in your notes the places you searched and failed to find your ancestors.

There are two file folders that make up the couples' file. One is the couples' manila file folder, which is dropped into one hanging surname file folder. The two files together are to be known as the couples' file. The reason for putting a manila file folder inside a hanging file folder is that a manila file folder by itself tends to slide down under other manila file folders. A hanging file folder will hold the manila file folder in place so you will be able to find it quickly.

The "Golden Rule" for research organization is to have a few rules and then obey the few.

Here are the "rules" for the Couples' File.

1 - Information on a direct-line ancestor goes into the couples' file folder when the couple gets married. The marriage certificate and related papers are the first papers to go into the couples' file.

2 - Information prior to the marriage goes into the parents file folder. For example , the children's birth certificates and baptism certificates are filed in the parent's couples' file.

3 - Organize all couples' file folders in alphabetical order by SURNAME.

4 - File or "put away" all documents you collect on a daily basis.

In order to help find a couple's file, set up the family lines in the file cabinet by positioning file tabs:

The file drawer needs to be set up in a way that will help the researcher find a needed file more efficiently. Filing quickly and accurately allows the researcher to work on other, more important work.

The couples' files may be arranged in one alphabetical sequence or broken into segments of alphabetically arranged files. Some prefer to keep all ancestral lines in one alphabetical arrangement so they don't have to remember to which part of their pedigree a particular surname belongs. Others arrange their files alphabetically, after dividing them by each grand parent surname.

The principles are the same in each approach. Since dividing the entire file by the grand parents line, we will describe that approach in the pages that follow.

The position of the vinyl tab will make it easier to find a family file. Setting up the hanging file folder with family lines can be done with the position of the vinyl tabs.

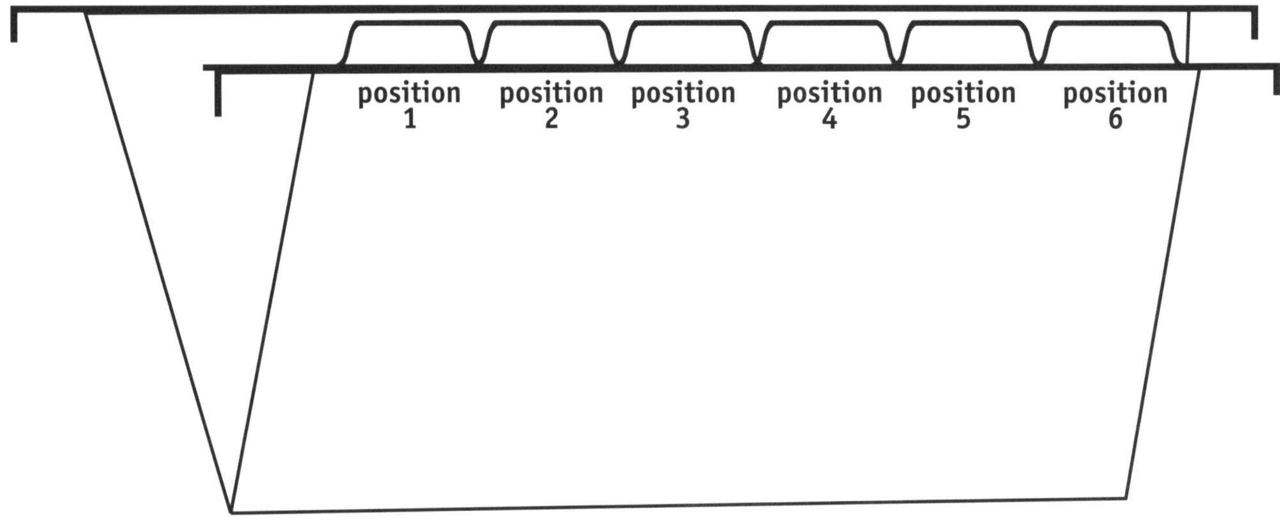

The legal file folders have six slots (without overlapping) across the top for 1/5 cut vinyl tabs. The letter size has five positions for 1/5 cut vinyl tabs. This list will indicate your family line by position (1 through 5 or 6).

1. Husband's Fathers line
2. Husband's Mothers line
3. Wife's Fathers line
4. Wife's Mothers line
5. Surname for a locality, Research Logs
6. Personal Stories
7. If you are using letter-sized folders, simply combine #'s 5 & 6.

The Position of Vinyl Tabs Will Indicate Your Ancestral Line

The position of the tabs will help you find your family ancestor. In order to simplify your file drawer, set up a "Master Surname Index File." The "Master Surname Index File" is a guide of color and position showing your four grandparents ancestral lines. The legal size has six positions and the letter sized has five-tab positions. The position of the SURNAME tab will identify your four grand parent ancestral lines (The four tab colors are blue, green, red and yellow).

Below is the "Master Surname Index File" with the vinyl tab headings. Here are the headings for the "Master Surname Index File" folder.

HUSBAND'S MOTHER	HUSBAND'S FATHER	WIFE'S FATHER	WIFE'S MOTHER	SURNAME FOR A LOCALITY	PERSONAL STORIES
LANGMAN	ALLEN	SMITH	WALKER	RESEARCH LOG	STORIES

It is suggested that a "Master Surname Index File" be put in front of the file drawer. The SURNAME hanging file folders need to be set up to hold the five or six tabs. Each position represents a direct or indirect ancestral family line. The first tab is the husband's father's line; the second tab is the husband's mother's line. The third tab is the wife's father's line and the fourth tab is the wife's mother's line.

Behind the Master Surname Index File, hang the rest of the file folders with the vinyl tab in the position of the ancestral line. Three vinyl tabs are to be set on the front side of the file folder and three tabs on the backside of the file folder. The reason for putting three on the front and three on the back is that all six will not fit on the front because of overlap.

Color codes may help you identify a SURNAME file, as follows:

BLUE GREEN RED YELLOW PURPLE PINK

SURNAME Hanging File Folders

Now, write the SURNAME of the husband along with his first name and put it on the vinyl tab of the hanging folder and put it in alphabetical order in the file cabinet.

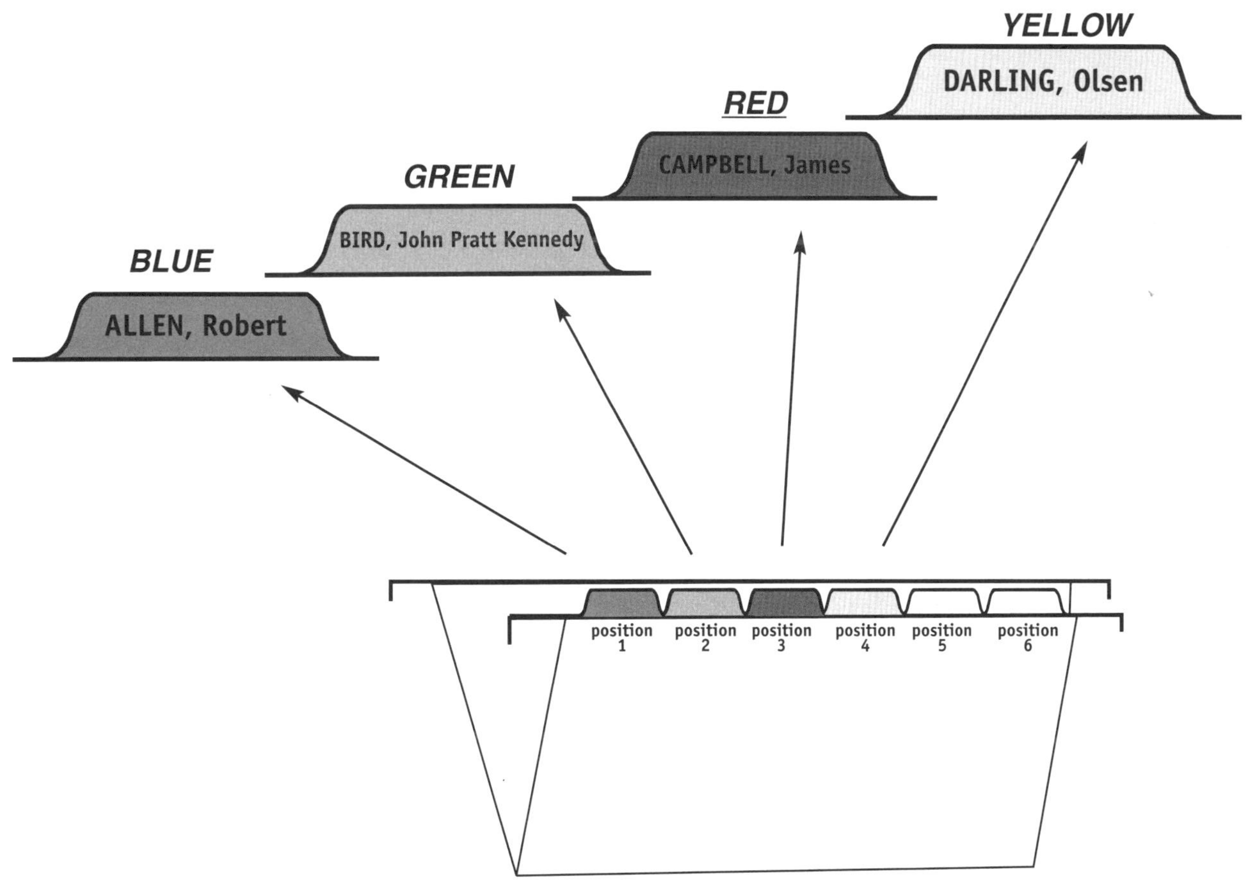

Manila File Folders

For each couple on the five- (5) generation and extended pedigree charts, make a manila file folder. Use the manila reinforced file folder with the 1/3 cut tab. Write the SURNAME of the husband, then his given name. To the right of the name put his birth date. Under the husband's name, write his wife's SURNAME, then her given name.

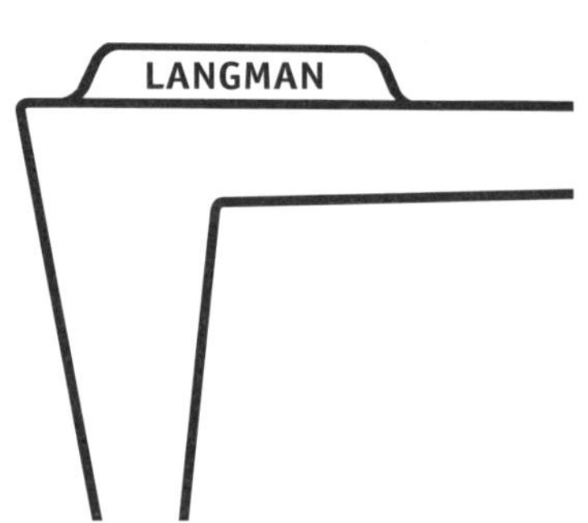

Then drop the manila folder into the hanging file folder (sometimes it is convenient to put two or three manila file folders into one hanging file folder). Manila file folders have a tendency to slide down into the file cabinet drawer.

The hanging file folder will hold the manila file folder in place. The double folder will keep the files in order.

Step 6:

Using a manila folder for a couple's file, put SURNAME and given name on tab and drop into a hanging file folder

Here is how the manila reinforced file folders tabs should look.

The couple's file is the combination of the manila file folder dropped in the hanging file folder

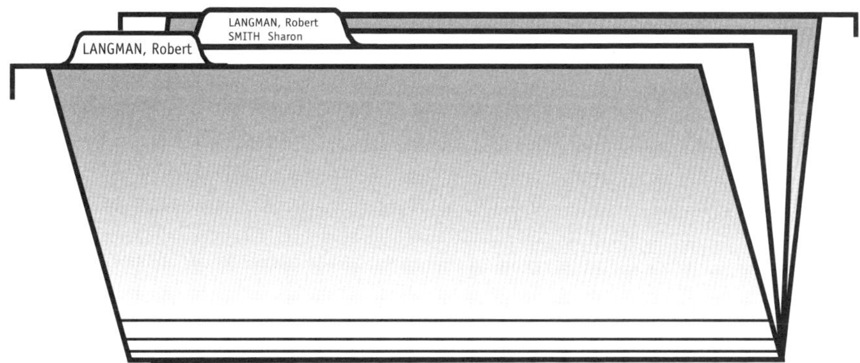

Hanging file folders along with a manila folder go into the top drawer of the file cabinet.

In summary, the hanging file folder will be put into the filing cabinet, the manila file folder is dropped into the SURNAME hanging file folder. This is done to store research records in an organized manner. The SURNAME hanging file folder and the manila file folder will now be known as the "Couple's File."

Step 7:

Assemble the documents and put them in a folder called "couple's file."

Chapter 4 Placing Copies of Original Documents into "Couple's Files"

Review from Chapter 3

1. Information about each family should be gathered and placed in a "Couples File" - - a manila folder with the name of the head of the family on it, placed inside a hanging folders.
2. "Couples' Files" should be organized alphabetically by SURNAME.

Set up a research file for each SURNAME on your pedigree charts:

There should be a couple's file for every couple on the five- (5) generation pedigree chart. As you extend your pedigree to additional charts, a file should also be organized with a pedigree, family group record; research notes, the research packet and copies of all documents.

Research objectives of genealogists are usually built around individuals or families. Sometimes a research objective concerns a locality or historical event. Your filing system should be flexible enough to accommodate any type of research objectives.

How to handle non-direct family names:

Most experts suggest that you research direct lines. However, there are a lot of non-direct families' names to deal with. For example, if your father has brothers and sisters, only your father is a direct line. It is important that his brothers and sisters be accounted for in your filing system. When you make a file for a non-direct line; put it in your file by SURNAME, in alphabetical order and show as brothers and sisters.

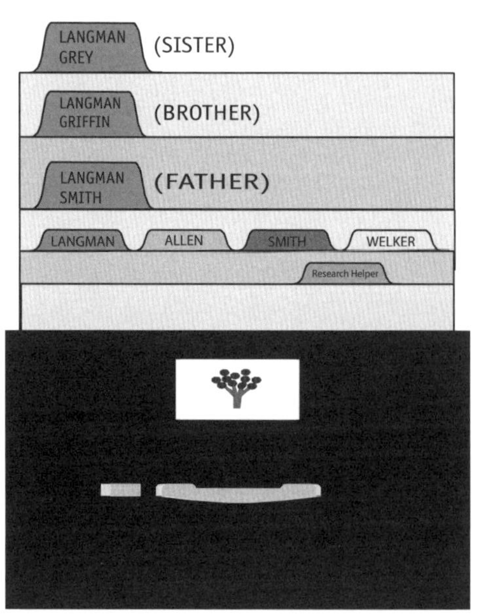

Put research helps and aids in front of filing drawer before couples' files

Often, there are research helps and research aids which apply to a broad spectrum of research. Place a copy of your research helps and aids in front of the couple's file (use the orange color vinyl tab for this file). Research helps are reference materials to be used in the future when you find other families in the same research area and research aids are visual aids.

Step 8:

Assemble Research Tools and drop them into the "couple's file"

Research Helps:

Here are examples of research helps:

History of Vigo, County, Indiana.
History of Franklin County, Massachusetts
History of Geauga County, Ohio

Language helps; Paleography; letter-writing guides; word lists & terminology.

Religion helps; religious history.

Examples of Research Helps files:

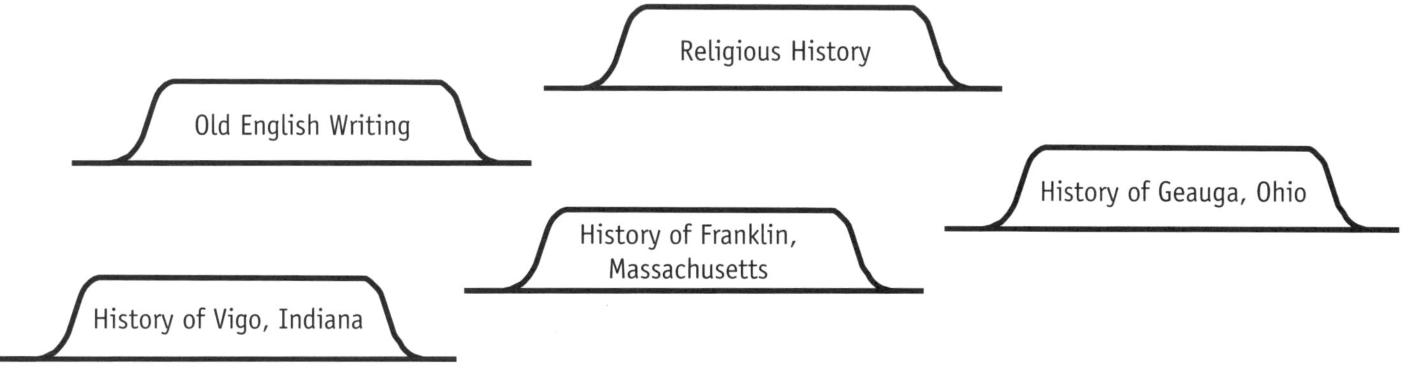

Research Aids:

Vigo country maps: Indiana.

Franklin County Massachusetts Maps

State maps: Indiana.

Coal Bluff City maps

Terre Haute City Map

Examples of Research Aids files:

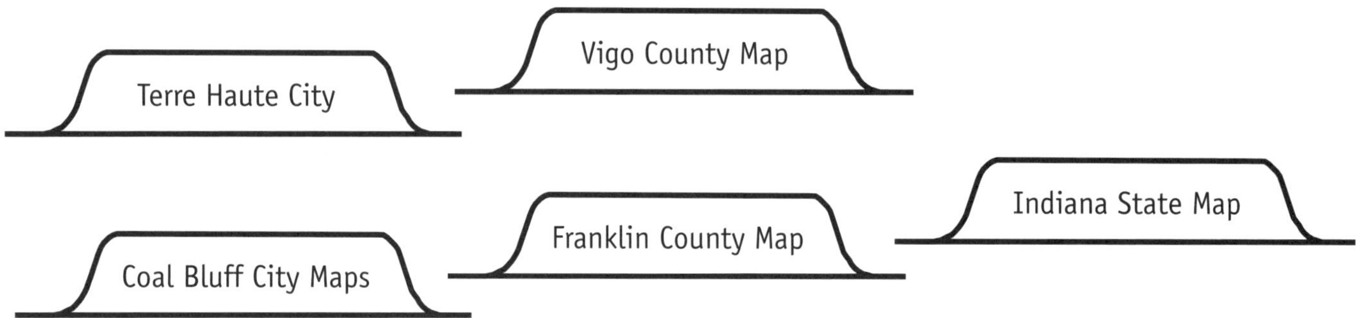

And thus, this is the moment to be organized.

This is a summary of how the file drawer should look. The file drawer should be set up in the following manner. In front of the file drawer, put in the "research aids and helps" file folders. Then place the "Master SURNAME Index Folder." The "Master SURNAME Index Folder" has five or six colored vinyl tabs and four of them will help identify your ancestral line. Finally, drop your couple's files into your filing cabinet and put them in alphabetical order by SURNAME.

Chapter 5 Tools To Help You Organize Your "Couple's File"

Review from Chapter 4

1. Tools to help you organize make genealogy efforts more efficient
   - The TO DO LIST is a place to record future research plans
   - The Research and Availability Checklist is a list of types of documents and sources available to meet research goals.
   - The Research Log is a place to record research as it is done and becomes a file of completed research results.
   - Other tools which are helpful are maps and time lines
2. These research tools are filed according to the focus of research or goal.

It is important for a genealogy researcher to use tools that help you organize.

Step 9:

The Couple's file will be organized in alphabetical order by surname

There is a tool for every job. In order to make the job more efficient, it is important to use the right tool. Tools that help you organize make the work more efficient. Please look over the following tools and review the definition for use.

Research Tools To put into "couples" file

-To Do List
-Research Checklist
-Research Log
-Time Line
-Maps

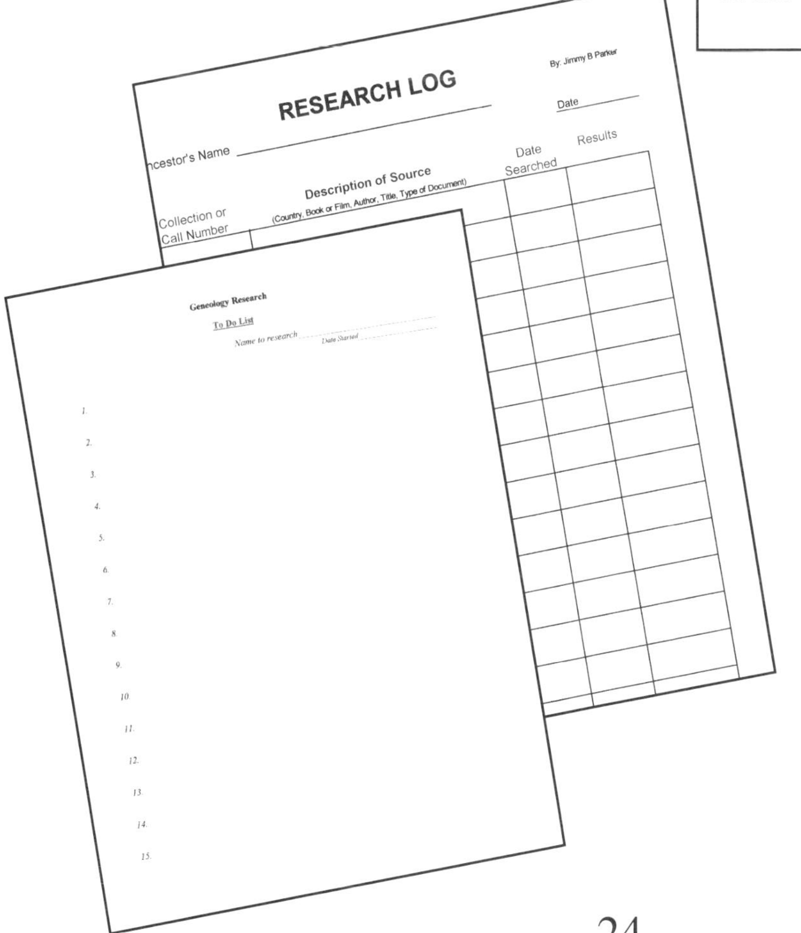

Robert R Langman, Ph D
84 West 7500 South
Midvale, Utah 84047
(801)568-0154

UNITED STATES
Research Checklist
Family Name______________________
Locality_________________________

SOURCE DOCUMENTS FOR RESEARCH

HOME

- ☐ Albums, Photographs
- ☐ Diaries, Journals
- ☐ Family Bible and Letters
- ☐ Internet
- ☐ Interviews
- ☐ Traditions

TOWN RECORDS

- ☐ Cemetery Records
- ☐ City or County Records
- ☐ Funeral Home Records
- ☐ Histories
- ☐ Newspaper Files
- ☐ Public School Records

COUNTY RECORDS

- ☐ Administration of Estates
- ☐ Civil & Criminal Court Records
- ☐ County Historical Society
- ☐ Deeds & Mortgages
- ☐ Militia Records
- ☐ Naturalization Tax and Voter's Lists
- ☐ Probate, Wills, Guardianships
- ☐ Sheriff's Sales
- ☐ Tax and Voter's Lists
- ☐ Vital Records: Birth/Marriage/Death

STATE RECORDS

- ☐ Accounts & Journals
- ☐ Homestead & Donation Land Claims
- ☐ Land Grants
- ☐ State Archives
- ☐ State Census
- ☐ State Historical Society
- ☐ Supreme & Appellate Court Records
- ☐ Vital Records

NATIONAL RECORDS

- ☐ Bounty Land Records
- ☐ Census (1790-1920)
- ☐ Circuit Court of Appeals
- ☐ District & Supreme Court Records
- ☐ Immigration Records
- ☐ Military Land Grants & Military Records
- ☐ Mortality Schedules - Census years
- ☐ National Archives
- ☐ National Historical Society
- ☐ Passenger Lists
- ☐ Pay Vouchers and Pension Records
- ☐ Public and Private Land Claims
- ☐ Vital Registration

LIBRARIES

- ☐ Biographical Compendia
- ☐ C D Pro-Phone
- ☐ Cemetery Records
- ☐ Church Records & Histories
- ☐ D A R Lineage Books
- ☐ D A R Patriot Index
- ☐ Directories to funeral homes&cemeteries
- ☐ Genealogies
- ☐ Interlibrary Loan
- ☐ Newspapers on Microfilm
- ☐ Obituary Collections and Indexes
- ☐ Printed and Manuscript Histories

Robert R Langman, Ph D
84 West 7500 South
Midvale, Utah 84047
(801)568-0154

UNITED STATES
Research Checklist
Family Name______________________
Locality_________________________

SOURCE DOCUMENTS FOR RESEARCH

HOME

- ☐ Albums, Photographs
- ☐ Diaries, Journals
- ☐ Family Bible and Letters
- ☐ Internet
- ☐ Interviews
- ☐ Traditions

TOWN RECORDS

- ☐ Cemetery Records
- ☐ City or County Records
- ☐ Funeral Home Records
- ☐ Histories
- ☐ Newspaper Files
- ☐ Public School Records

COUNTY RECORDS

- ☐ Administration of Estates
- ☐ Civil & Criminal Court Records
- ☐ County Historical Society
- ☐ Deeds & Mortgages
- ☐ Militia Records
- ☐ Naturalization Tax and Voter's Lists
- ☐ Probate, Wills, Guardianships
- ☐ Sheriff's Sales
- ☐ Tax and Voter's Lists
- ☐ Vital Records: Birth/Marriage/Death

STATE RECORDS

- ☐ Accounts & Journals
- ☐ Homestead & Donation Land Claims
- ☐ Land Grants
- ☐ State Archives
- ☐ State Census
- ☐ State Historical Society
- ☐ Supreme & Appellate Court Records
- ☐ Vital Records

NATIONAL RECORDS

- ☐ Bounty Land Records
- ☐ Census (1790-1920)
- ☐ Circuit Court of Appeals
- ☐ District & Supreme Court Records
- ☐ Immigration Records
- ☐ Military Land Grants & Military Records
- ☐ Mortality Schedules - Census years
- ☐ National Archives
- ☐ National Historical Society
- ☐ Passenger Lists
- ☐ Pay Vouchers and Pension Records
- ☐ Public and Private Land Claims
- ☐ Vital Registration

LIBRARIES

- ☐ Biographical Compendia
- ☐ C D Pro-Phone
- ☐ Cemetery Records
- ☐ Church Records & Histories
- ☐ D A R Lineage Books
- ☐ D A R Patriot Index
- ☐ Directories to funeral homes&cemeteries
- ☐ Genealogies
- ☐ Interlibrary Loan
- ☐ Newspapers on Microfilm
- ☐ Obituary Collections and Indexes
- ☐ Printed and Manuscript Histories

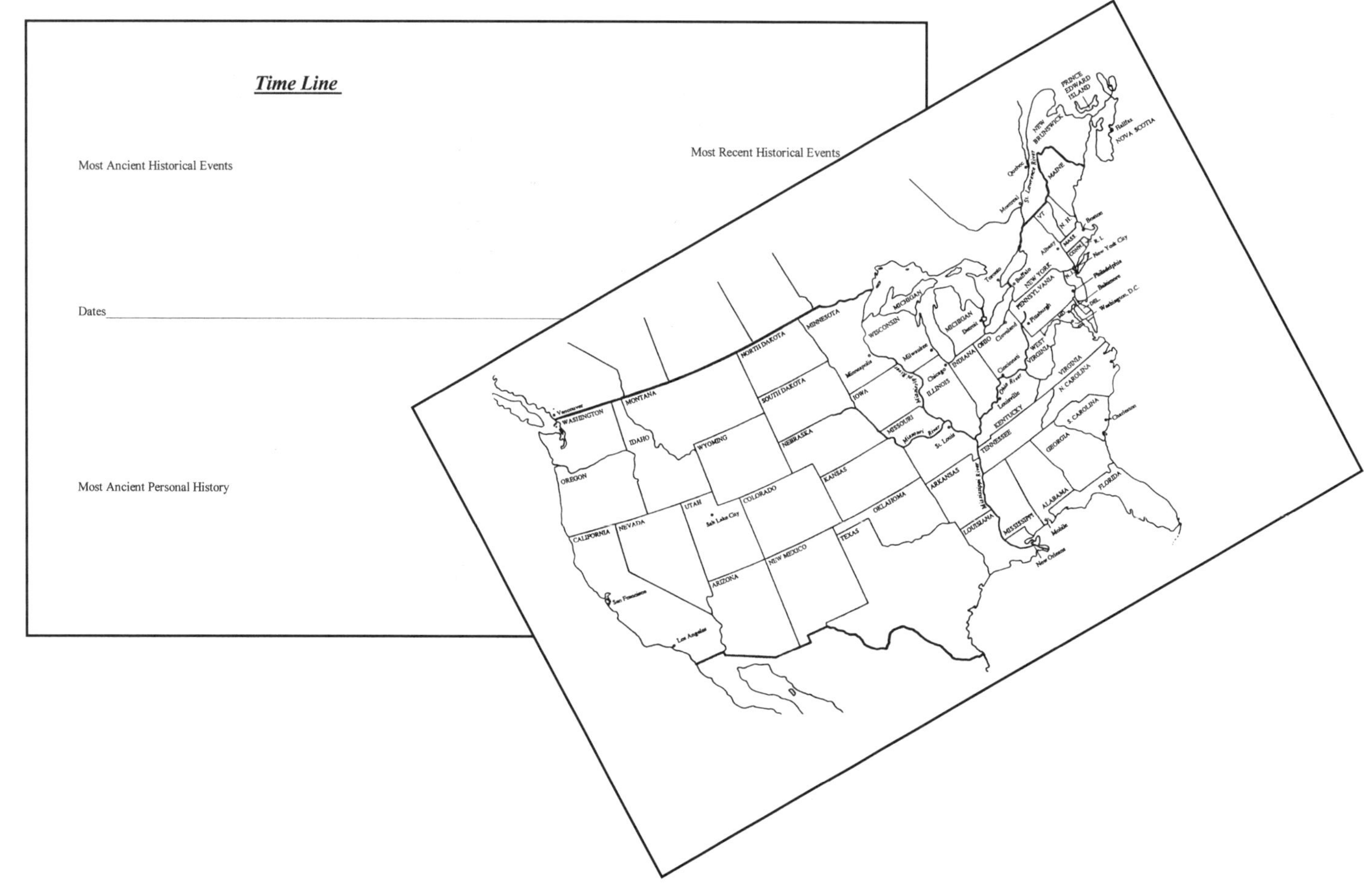

Time Line

Most Ancient Historical Events

Most Recent Historical Events

Dates_____________________________

Most Ancient Personal History

Tools to Help You Organize Make Genealogy Work Efforts More Efficient

1 - The "To Do List" includes notations made of future research to be performed. This can be filled out at any time and at any place, especially when ideas come to mind (See illustration on page 70).

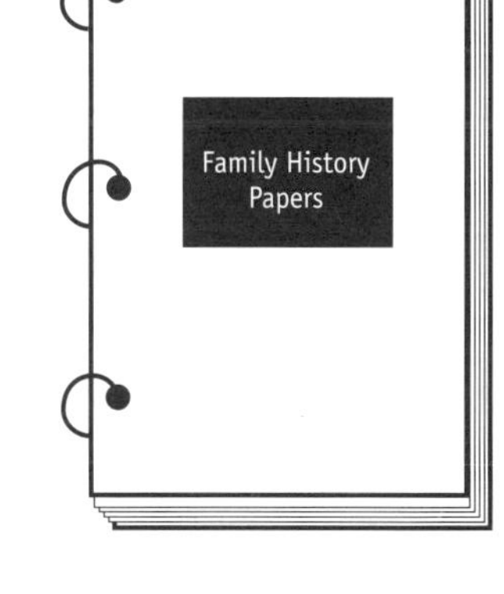

2 - The Research and Availability Checklist is a list of all types of documents and paper sources. This checklist is to be used in order to help find the needed genealogy information that will help prove the existence of an individual. When a document has been researched, check off each item as it was searched. This is done to avoid research duplication. The list will also be a reminder of research that still needs to be done. Also, included on the research checklist is an Availability by Century Chart (The chart is found on the right half of the checklist form). The purpose for this chart is to alert the researcher of the historical dates the document actually existed (See illustration on pages 71 & 72).

Step 10:

Set up a section in the filing system for research *helps* and *aids*

3 - The Research Log is a record of past research completed with references and sources and also can be used to take research notes while in the library. This log can be put into your notes, the SURNAME file, the research folders by locality, or a separate file for your logs. (See illustration on page 74).

4 - Maps of the area being researched should be included, (Example, country, state, county, township or cities) (see illustration on page 75).

5 - The Time Line is a research tool that will help locate information. This is to be filled out to compare the individual events with historical events. This comparison should bring forth date and place clues for investigation (See illustration on page73).

An Old Chinese proverb says: "If you see turtle on a fence, you know someone put it there." *-Anonymous*

Now, here is what you do with the pile of all those documents and papers. If you want to find papers in your file, then you need to put them there. Put away your papers in the same order for each file. "A file for everything and everything in its file."

Your Research May Determine Where You File It.

Sometimes research is done on an individual. Sometimes the focus of research is a family group. And sometimes the researcher wants to focus on all persons of a particular surname in a locality. Research sometimes is even done on the history of a locality where several ancestral families may have resided. The focus of research will determine where the to do lists, research logs, maps and time lines are filed.

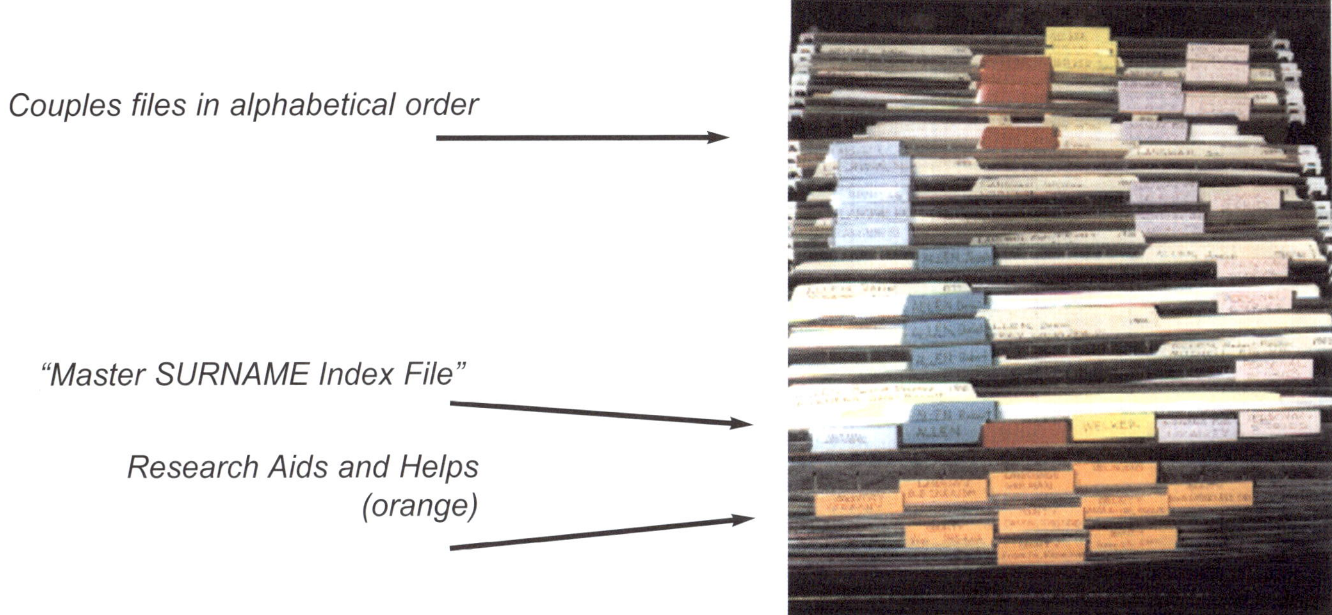

The first four colored tabs are SURNAME file folders

First row (blue) is the Langman line, second row (green) is the Allen Line, third row (red) is the Smith line, forth row (yellow) is the Walker line, fifth row (purple) is for research by locality and sixth Row (personal stories). In front (orange) is research aids and helps.

Chapter 6 Reviewing the Ten Steps To Organization

Review from Chapter 5:

1. Organize the information you have gathered into files for each couple on your pedigree chart.
2. Include in each couple's file, a copy of the pedigree chart, a copy of the couple's family group record, and other information gathered through research.

In summary, there are ten steps to set up a genealogy filing system.

Organization will inspire a genealogy researcher to continue their work. It is true that when you organize your genealogy properly, you will continue to maintain your interest and the research will thrive. You will be a "doer" of research rather than just a "talker." The organization in this presentation includes a simple but complete family history system that will allow you to find any document or paper quickly.

1. - Put all loose papers and documents into one place, and sort by SURNAME.
2. - Using the computer, enter data into your data management program and create a family group record and notes. Take the information from the papers and documents you have collected.
3. - Make or Print (if you use a computer)a pedigree chart. A pedigree chart is like the table of contents in a book. It will guide you to your family group records (in the computer, data entered on the family group record will copy on the pedigree chart).
4. - Using hanging file folders make a SURNAME file. Attach a vinyl tab and insert a slip of paper with your SURNAME.

5. - On the hanging file folder place the vinyl tab in a position that will indicate the family ancestral line.

6. - Make a couple's file, using a 1/3 cut manila file folder. On the manila file folder tab, print the husband's SURNAME, given name and birth date. Directly under his name is the wife's SURNAME(maiden) and given name then drop the manila folder into the hanging file folder. The two files now become one file called the couple's file.

7. - Assemble documents and put into file. Place in the proper couple's files. The first document should be a pedigree chart, a family group record, and your notes. Then follow with your primary documents, (like a birth certificates) and secondary documents, (like a census index). Also, include all other documents and photos.

8. - Assemble tools to help you organize and drop into couples' files (the tools consists of a To Do List, a Research Checklist, a Map, a Research Log and a Time Line).

9. - The Couple's file folder will be filed in alphabetical order by SURNAME of the husband, then given names.

10. - Set up a section in the filing system for research helps (like research papers on churches) and aids (like a city map).

All this should be done in an orderly manner so that any paper can be found "within 30 Seconds."

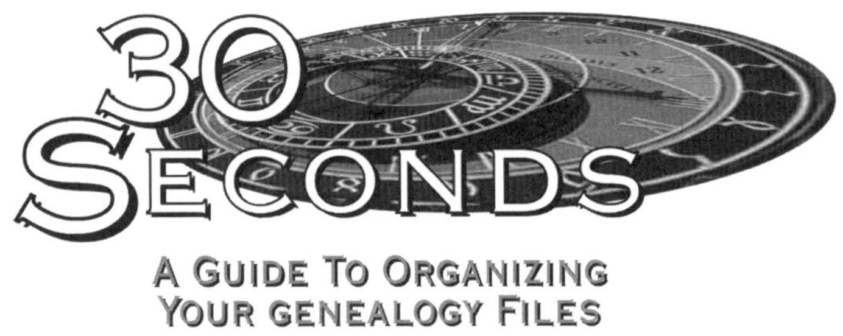

Part 2, Organizing Your Genealogy Notebook Filing System

Chapter 7 How You Succeed in Your Notebook Filing System

Review from Chapter 6

1. Organizing your research files will assist you in genealogy
2. Using ten steps to set up your filing cabinet system

"It wasn't raining when Noah built the ark." *-Howard Ruff 1930*

It is never too late to start organizing your genealogy. It is best to start when there is no pressure because when it "rains" the pressure is on. The reason for using a notebook filing system is that notebooks are very convenient to use. This notebook filing system will be used because of your personal preference. If this system matches your personality it is the best system.

Genealogy is becoming a very popular hobby throughout the world. Many people are becoming totally involved in this pastime. For some, it becomes a passion. Therefore, a simple organization of documents and papers is essential. The goal is to pursue your passion with confidence and success. Becoming organized will bring confidence. Setting up an organized genealogy system is of great assistance in finding ancestors. The organizational system you choose needs to be simple to set up, it must be easy to maintain. It must be flexible and easy to use.

"If Columbus had an advisory committee he would probably still be at the dock."
-Justice Arthur Goldberg 1908 - 1990

Take courage and decide how you want to organize your genealogy papers. You can talk to a lot of people and each person will give you a different method of organizing your genealogy. Some will tell you not to worry about organizing your genealogy. It is time to make a decision and select the best system that will help you. Your goal is to have an organized system that will make it easy for you to find the papers you need.

"So the service of the house...was set in order" *-2 Chronicles 29:35*

Preserving your personal paper documents is so important that some people keep them in a safe. Keeping your records, documents and certificates in a safe place is important. Many genealogy researchers put them in quality notebooks and store them in a safe, dry place. If they do this in an organized and orderly manner, their family history house will be put in order. The goal is to preserve your genealogy papers and have them in order.

"Let all things be done decently and in order." *-1 Corinthians 14:40*

Step 1:

Put paper and documents into one place by surname

It is possible to have a predictable and an well-organized notebook filing system.

Here is how your Notebook filing system should look when you are finished.

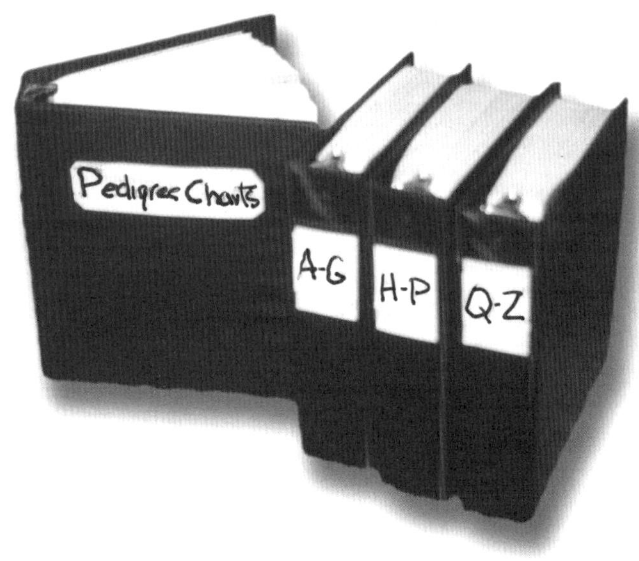

There are two notebooks. The first is a notebook of pedigree charts. A pedigree chart is like a table of contents in a book, it assists in finding your ancestor's name, date and place. This notebook system uses a numerical system that will help you easily find the pedigree chart you would like.

In the upper right hand corner is the number of the pedigree chart. The first pedigree chart is number one so in the upper right hand corner is the number 1. Down the right side of the pedigree chart are 16 spaces for numbers (2 through 17). Below number one is number 2. Chart number 1 extends to chart number 2.

The second notebook contains your family group records. Your family group records need to be inserted into your notebooks in alphabetical order by surname. This can be done by using a set of insertable dividers. The insertable dividers need to be put in alphabetical order (A through Z). Behind the dividers the following papers are placed. The sequence of papers are these, the first paper is the pedigree chart, then a family group record, followed by your notes, primary documents and secondary documents. After these documents include your tools that will help you organize and to find your research information.

"Master Surname Index Divider"

In front of the family group record notebook, is a "Master Surname Index Divider." The "Master Surname Index Divider" holds all the colored tabs and shows the position and color (see color in example) of your ancestral lines.

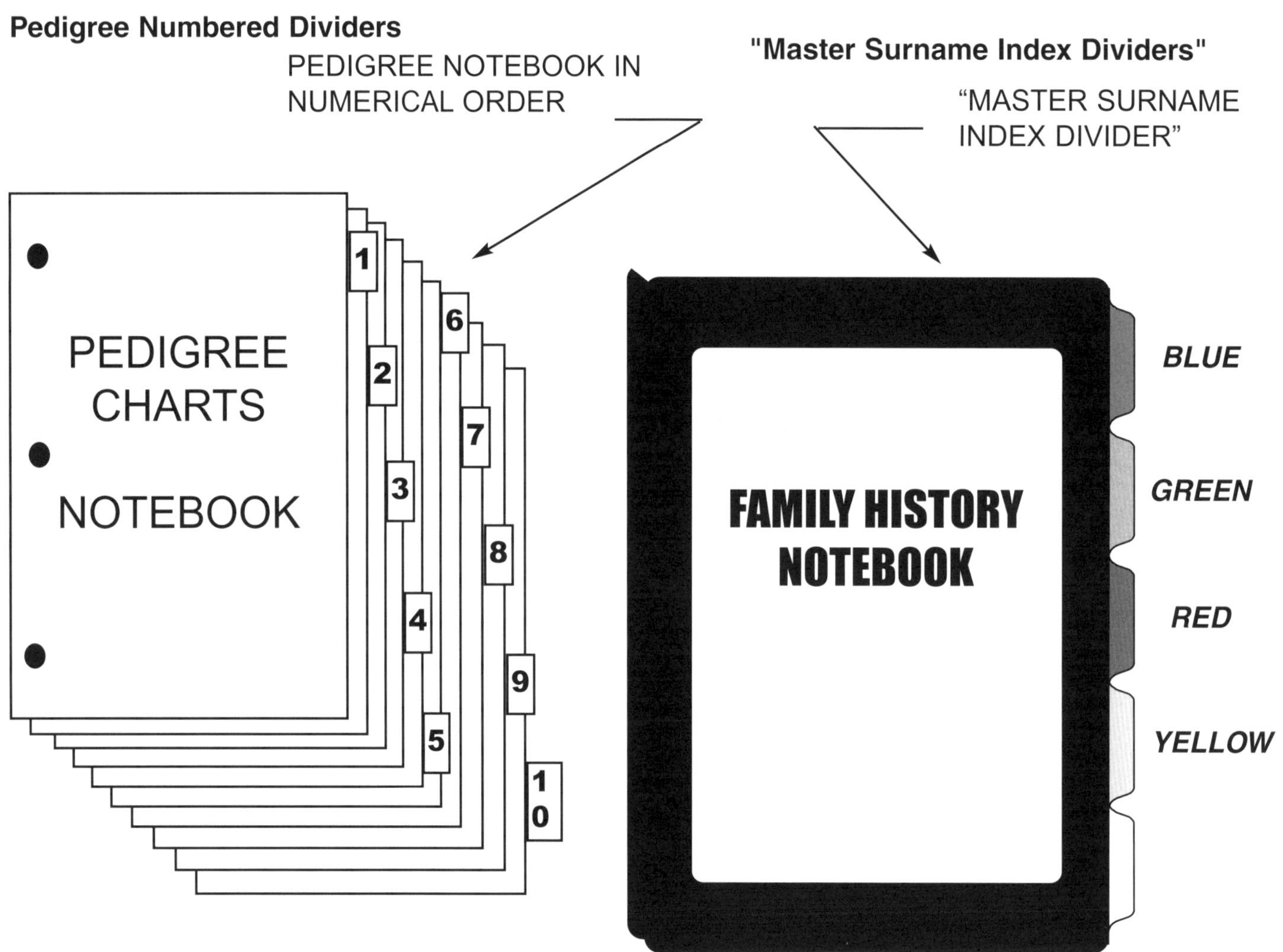

Chapter 8 You Need Two Sets of Notebooks:

Review from Chapter 7

1. It is never too late to start organizing your notebook filing system
2. When you put your genealogy in order, you will be able to find it.
3. The use of two notebooks is needed for your pedigree charts and family group records
4. Use a set of numerical insertable dividers for your pedigree charts and a set of alphabetical insertable dividers for your family group sheets.

"It is quality rather than quantity that matters." *-Seneca, Epistles 45, 1*

Select three ring, 2" quality notebooks that you like for your genealogy. Quality notebooks are needed so that the rings will close securely and align properly.

Step 2:

Create two sets of notebooks for pedigree and family group records

You will develop two types of notebooks: (1) a notebook of pedigree charts and (2) several notebooks for family group records, notes and all other documents.

The first notebook will hold all your pedigree charts, filed in numerical order. You will need to use a practical numbering system. Several additional notebooks may be needed to file all your family group records and notes by SURNAME in alphabetical order.

An example of pedigree charts and family group records in notebooks:

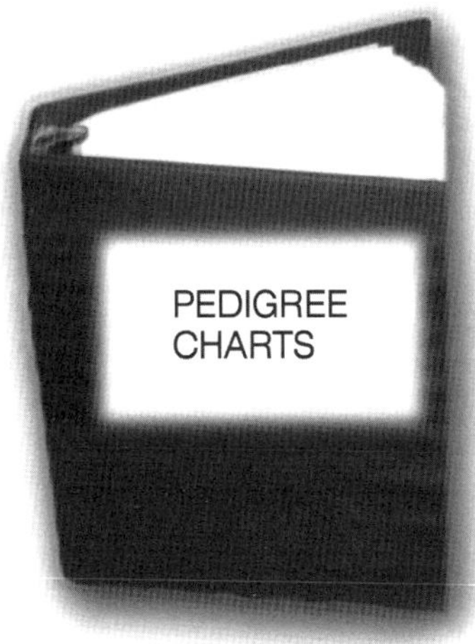

For this presentation, the computer data management program will be used to print documents

The computer is a much awaited genealogy research medium. The computer will be used to print pedigree charts, family group records and notes.

"It's always been and always will be the same in the world: The horse does all the work and the coachman is tipped." *-Anonymous*

Genealogy researchers do the work. Some are very talented and work hard. They want the work to go on and be done exactly and completely. They ask for no reward (tips) but work to see accurate results. They seek no attention but work to accomplish a task. Those who are organized do their basic research well. Their work is complete and accurate. Let's continue our to organize our notebooks.

Using the computer, enter data into your genealogy data management program. Print a pedigree chart, family group record and notes.

1. - Print your pedigree charts with five generations. The pedigree chart ties the direct line generations together, i.e., son to father, father to grandfather and so on as far back as you can. (See illustration on page 65).

2. - Make up family group records showing parents with children. Enter the SURNAME, given names, dates and places for births, marriages and deaths. (See illustration page 66 & 67.

3. -Research notes is a place in which to put research notations. It includes the detailed notes of all research done in the past along with present notations. Any future plans of research should also be noted. Detailed notes should include all appropriate annotations and document sources (including all research that did not provide results). Any genealogy researcher should be able to go to into your notes and understand the status of your research because your notes will explain. It is important to know the status of your research, so write everything you do in your notes (be sure to include all negative searches completed). If your notes are complete and well documented then other researchers will be less likely duplicate your work. (See illustration page 68 & 69).

Enter data into your computer and print your pedigree chart, family group records and notes.

Enter data into Computer, Print your papers:
-Pedigree Chart
-Family Group Records
-Research Notes

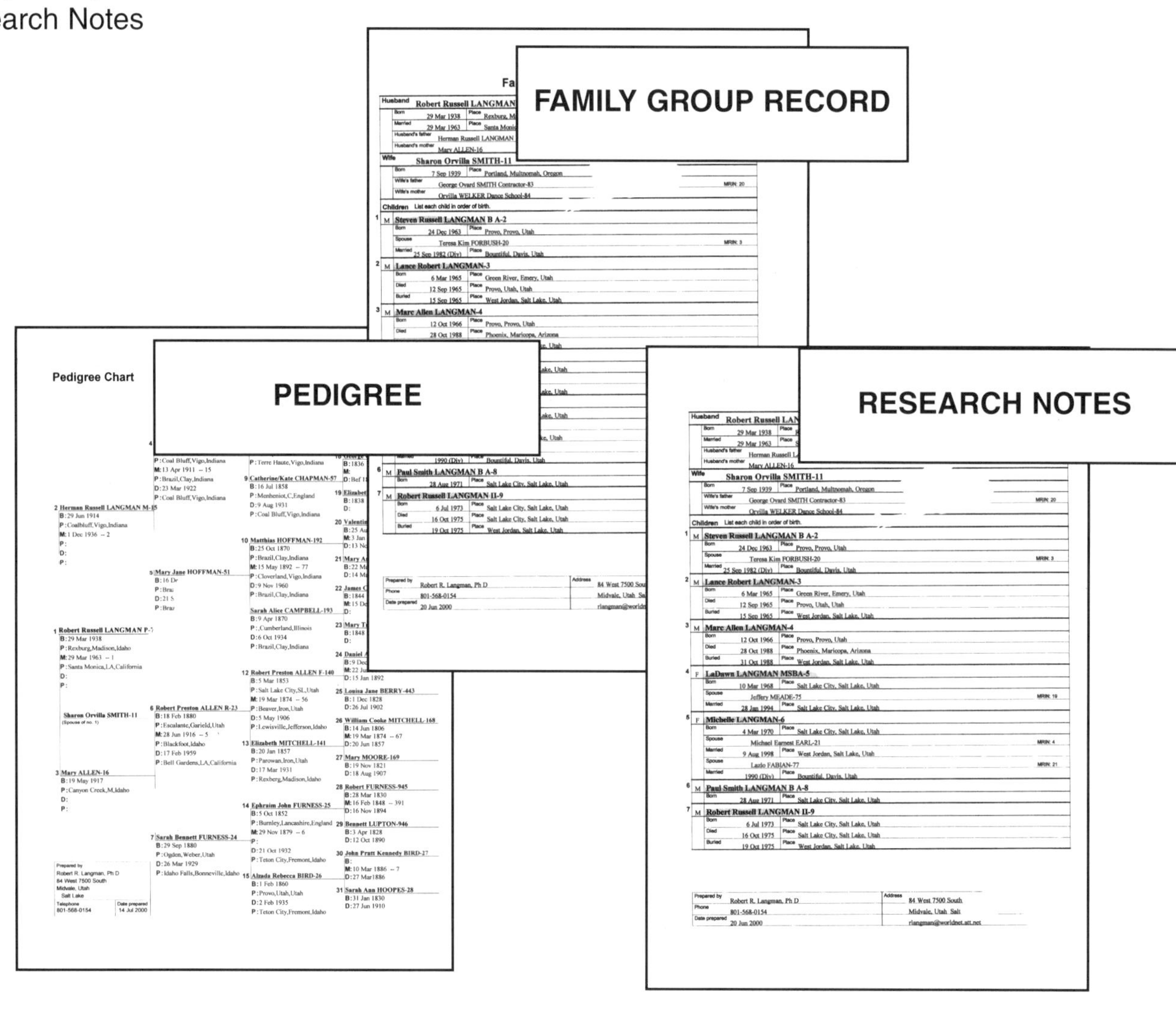

Supplies:

The following supplies are needed to set up your notebook filing system:

-At least three 2", 3 ring notebooks (in which you place papers and documents)

-Notebook tags which will show the description of the notebooks (will help find binders with a "quick look").

-81/2" x 11" computer paper for printing records

-Sheet protectors, polypropylene acid free, non-stick (used to store and protect documents)

-An 81/2" x 11" notebook with acid-free paper. (to be used for note taking and to record ideas)

-Glue and stickers, acid free (used to secure papers, pictures, drawings and notes)

-A set of insertable dividers with numerical tabs (used to put pedigree chart in numerical order).

-A set of alphabetical indexes (A - Z). (used to place family group records in alphabetical order).

-Several sets of insertable dividers 81/2" X 11" with clear tabs (to be used to identify surnames)

-Large pedigree chart to hang on the wall (for a quick visual reference to generations and their relationships)

Review from Chapter 8

1. This notebook filing system presented here is an example of a system that works very well.
2. Learn notebook organizational principles and techniques
3. Develop a notebook filing system using two sets of notebooks.

"In organization there is always strength..." *-George Matthew Adams*

Put genealogy papers and documents in a pile on your desk, i.e., birth, marriage and death certificates, documents, pictures, and letters, family histories and notes about relatives.

langman allen walker smith

Family History Papers

Divide up all your papers and documents and organize them by SURNAME.

Divide all your papers and documents you have gathered. Separate all the documents into piles by SURNAME. Put materials together by SURNAME.

Put your filing system things in order.

Place a complete set of alphanumerical tabs (A to Z) in the notebook. You will place all your documents, in alphabetical order, behind your alphabetized tabs. You should file by SURNAME, given name and then date.

Step 3:

Two sets of Insertable dividers, one numerical, the second alphabetical

When you put your four sets of insertable dividers in your notebook use clear vinyl tabs:

These insertable dividers are in your notebook to help identify the couples by SURNAME. Print your SURNAMES on a colored (see example below) paper tab and insert it into the clear vinyl tabs on your insertable dividers.

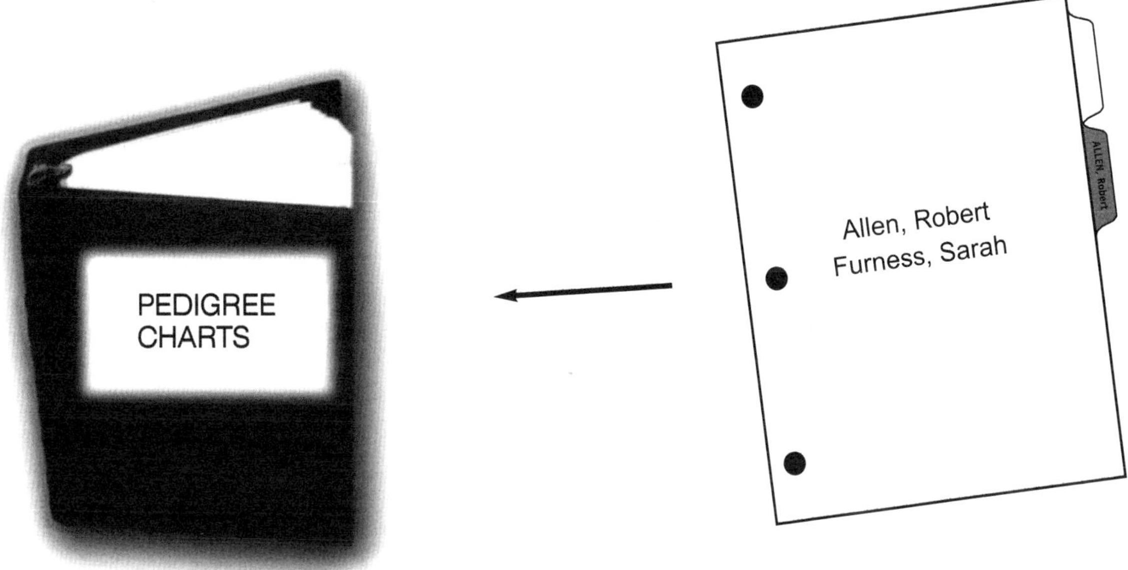

The position and alignment of vinyl tabs on insertable dividers will indicate the parent's ancestry.

Setting up the insertable dividers with family lines can be done by assigning a family line to the position and alignment of the clear vinyl tabs. The insertable dividers have five tabs down the side, the first four will be used to identify your ancestral lines.

1. Husband's Fathers line
2. Husband's Mothers line
3. Wife's Fathers line
4. Wife's Mothers line
5. Research Notes by Locality and Personal Life Stories

The position of the clear vinyl tab will indicate which ancestral line you are following:

Each position represents a direct ancestral family line. The first tab is the Husband's father's line; the second tab is the husband's mother's line. The third tab is the wife's father's tab and the fourth tab is the wife's mother's tab.

Step 4:

Alphabetical insertable dividers with position and color to show ancestral lines

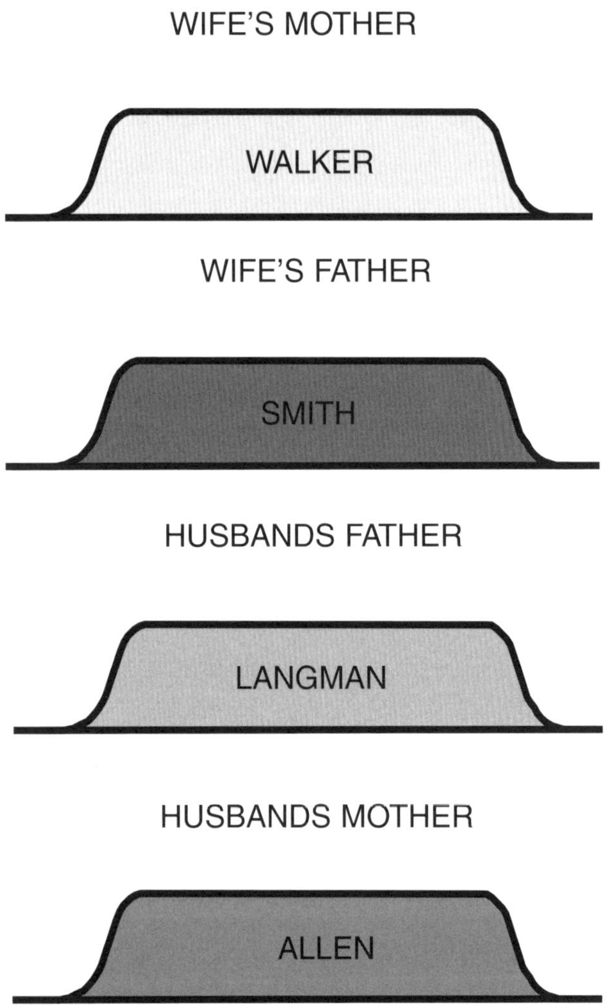

The position of clear vinyl tabs on the insertable dividers will determine your ancestor's line.

WIFE'S MOTHER

WALKER

WIFE'S FATHER

SMITH

HUSBANDS FATHER

LANGMAN

HUSBANDS MOTHER

ALLEN

FAMILY HISTORY NOTEBOOK

The notebook insertable dividers has room for five vinyl tabs down the side. It is recommended that a "Master Surname Index Divider" be put in front of the genealogy records notebook and be set up to hold all four tabs. Behind the "Master Surname Index Divider," assemble the rest of the alphabetized tab inserts to represent your ancestral lines. It will act as a guide to quickly identify your ancestral lines.

You may want to add color to help identify the ancestral line you want

You will be able to identify four family lines by viewing the position of the clear vinyl tabs, this may be further clarified by color. Write the SURNAME on a colored tab insert. The colored tab insert is a piece of colored paper that will fit into the clear vinyl tab. The paper is cut to size, then slipped into the tab. This is done to help identify a family ancestral line.

Use a color code that will help you identify a SURNAME file, use the colors as follows:

BLUE GREEN RED YELLOW

Put SURNAME Insertable Divider Tabs In Alphabetical Order.

Now, write the SURNAME of the husband along with his given name on the colored paper and slide it into the clear vinyl tab. Put the colored tabs in alphabetical order.

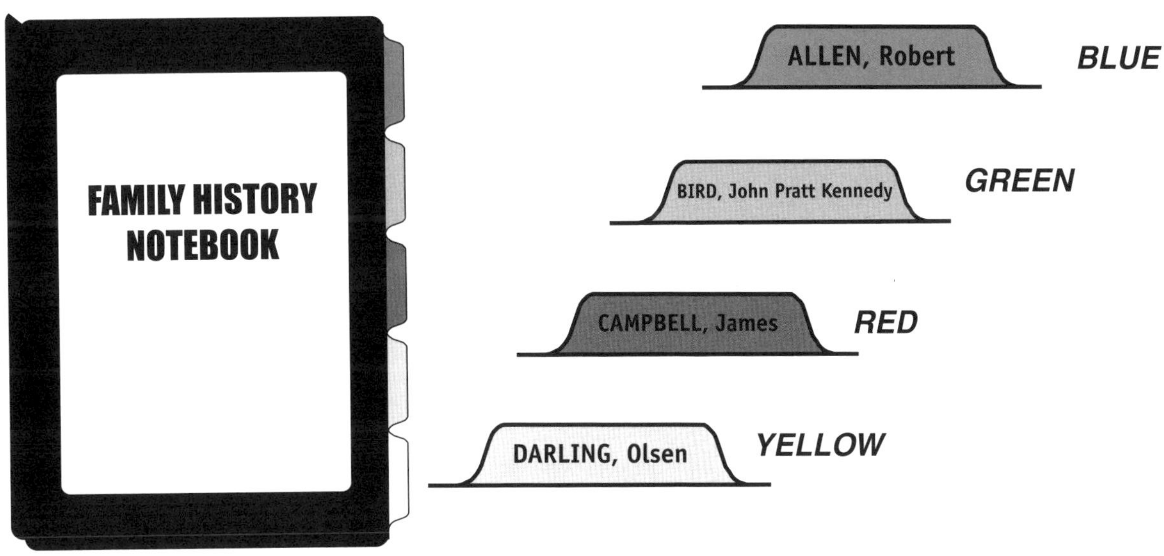

Here is how the family group record should look

Fill-in your family group record with names, dates and places for husband wife and children.

Step 5:

Print Pedigree Charts, Family Group Records and Notes

Fill-in Family Group Record

-Enter names, dates places for Husband, Wife & Children

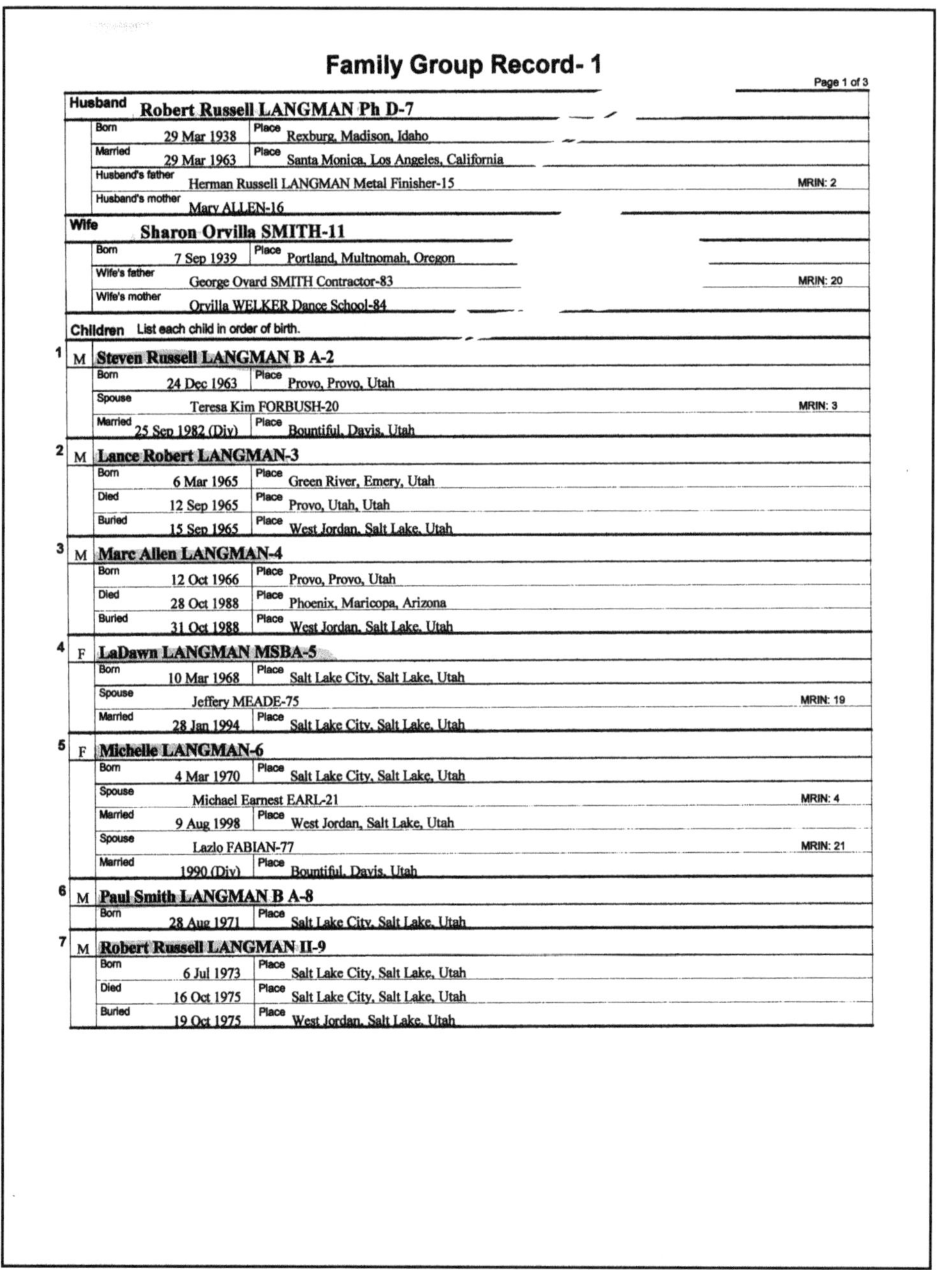

Family Group Record- 1

Page 1 of 3

Husband Robert Russell LANGMAN Ph D-7

Born	29 Mar 1938	Place	Rexburg, Madison, Idaho
Married	29 Mar 1963	Place	Santa Monica, Los Angeles, California
Husband's father	Herman Russell LANGMAN Metal Finisher-15		MRIN: 2
Husband's mother	Mary ALLEN-16		

Wife Sharon Orvilla SMITH-11

Born	7 Sep 1939	Place	Portland, Multnomah, Oregon
Wife's father	George Ovard SMITH Contractor-83		MRIN: 20
Wife's mother	Orvilla WELKER Dance School-84		

Children List each child in order of birth.

1 M **Steven Russell LANGMAN B A-2**

Born	24 Dec 1963	Place	Provo, Provo, Utah
Spouse	Teresa Kim FORBUSH-20		MRIN: 3
Married	25 Sep 1982 (Div)	Place	Bountiful, Davis, Utah

2 M **Lance Robert LANGMAN-3**

Born	6 Mar 1965	Place	Green River, Emery, Utah
Died	12 Sep 1965	Place	Provo, Utah, Utah
Buried	15 Sep 1965	Place	West Jordan, Salt Lake, Utah

3 M **Marc Allen LANGMAN-4**

Born	12 Oct 1966	Place	Provo, Provo, Utah
Died	28 Oct 1988	Place	Phoenix, Maricopa, Arizona
Buried	31 Oct 1988	Place	West Jordan, Salt Lake, Utah

4 F **LaDawn LANGMAN MSBA-5**

Born	10 Mar 1968	Place	Salt Lake City, Salt Lake, Utah
Spouse	Jeffery MEADE-75		MRIN: 19
Married	28 Jan 1994	Place	Salt Lake City, Salt Lake, Utah

5 F **Michelle LANGMAN-6**

Born	4 Mar 1970	Place	Salt Lake City, Salt Lake, Utah
Spouse	Michael Earnest EARL-21		MRIN: 4
Married	9 Aug 1998	Place	West Jordan, Salt Lake, Utah
Spouse	Lazlo FABIAN-77		MRIN: 21
Married	1990 (Div)	Place	Bountiful, Davis, Utah

6 M **Paul Smith LANGMAN B A-8**

Born	28 Aug 1971	Place	Salt Lake City, Salt Lake, Utah

7 M **Robert Russell LANGMAN II-9**

Born	6 Jul 1973	Place	Salt Lake City, Salt Lake, Utah
Died	16 Oct 1975	Place	Salt Lake City, Salt Lake, Utah
Buried	19 Oct 1975	Place	West Jordan, Salt Lake, Utah

Chapter 10 "By the Numbers"

Review from Chapter 9

1. Organize papers for notebook filing system
2. Put insertable dividers into your notebook
3. Assign position and color of tabs which indicate ancestral lines
4. Make family group records

Fill in your Pedigree Charts:

When you have filled in all the pedigree charts you can then print them. Don't be in a hurry, enter your information carefully. Start with yourself and go back as far as you can.

Put Family Pedigree Charts in Numerical order, Then put them into your notebook.

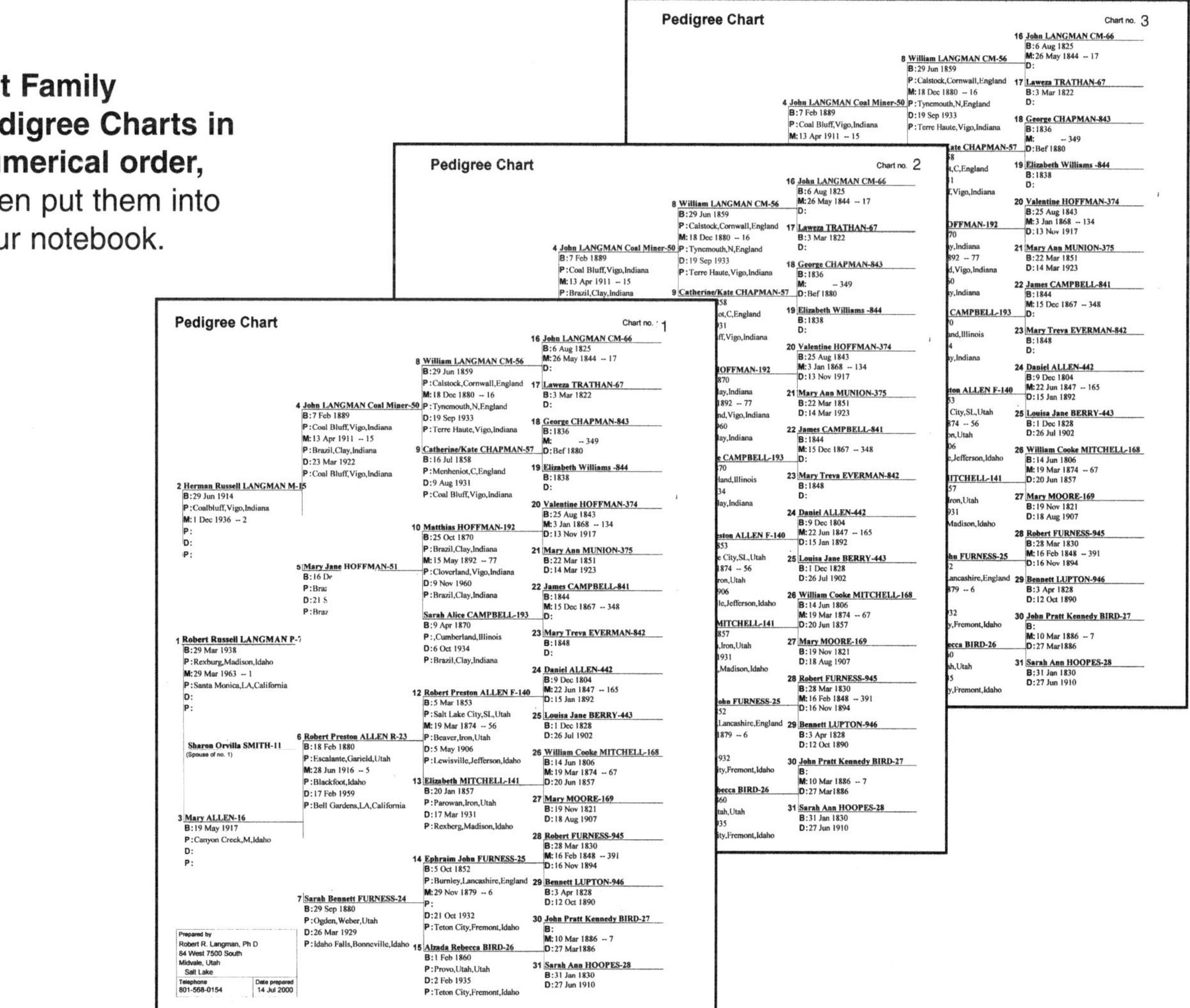

Pedigree Chart — Chart no. 3

Pedigree Chart — Chart no. 2

Pedigree Chart — Chart no. 1

1 Robert Russell LANGMAN P-7
B: 29 Mar 1938
P: Rexburg, Madison, Idaho
M: 29 Mar 1963 -- 1
P: Santa Monica, LA, California
D:
P:

Sharon Orvilla SMITH-11 (Spouse of no. 1)

2 Herman Russell LANGMAN M-15
B: 29 Jun 1914
P: Coalbluff, Vigo, Indiana
M: 1 Dec 1936 -- 2
P:
D:
P:

3 Mary ALLEN-16
B: 19 May 1917
P: Canyon Creek, M, Idaho
D:
P:

4 John LANGMAN Coal Miner-50
B: 7 Feb 1889
P: Coal Bluff, Vigo, Indiana
M: 13 Apr 1911 -- 15
P: Brazil, Clay, Indiana
D: 23 Mar 1922
P: Coal Bluff, Vigo, Indiana

5 Mary Jane HOFFMAN-51
B: 16 De
P: Bra
D: 21 S
P: Braz

6 Robert Preston ALLEN R-23
B: 18 Feb 1880
P: Escalante, Garield, Utah
M: 28 Jun 1916 -- 5
P: Blackfoot, Idaho
D: 17 Feb 1959
P: Bell Gardens, LA, California

7 Sarah Bennett FURNESS-24
B: 29 Sep 1880
P: Ogden, Weber, Utah
D: 26 Mar 1929
P: Idaho Falls, Bonneville, Idaho

8 William LANGMAN CM-56
B: 29 Jun 1859
P: Calstock, Cornwall, England
M: 18 Dec 1880 -- 16
P: Tynemouth, N, England
D: 19 Sep 1933
P: Terre Haute, Vigo, Indiana

9 Catherine/Kate CHAPMAN-57
B: 16 Jul 1858
P: Menheniot, C, England
D: 9 Aug 1931
P: Coal Bluff, Vigo, Indiana

10 Matthias HOFFMAN-192
B: 25 Oct 1870
P: Brazil, Clay, Indiana
M: 15 May 1892 -- 77
P: Cloverland, Vigo, Indiana
D: 9 Nov 1960
P: Brazil, Clay, Indiana

Sarah Alice CAMPBELL-193
B: 9 Apr 1870
P: , Cumberland, Illinois
D: 6 Oct 1934
P: Brazil, Clay, Indiana

12 Robert Preston ALLEN F-140
B: 5 Mar 1853
P: Salt Lake City, SL, Utah
M: 19 Mar 1874 -- 56
P: Beaver, Iron, Utah
D: 5 May 1906
P: Lewisville, Jefferson, Idaho

13 Elizabeth MITCHELL-141
B: 20 Jan 1857
P: Parowan, Iron, Utah
D: 17 Mar 1931
P: Rexberg, Madison, Idaho

14 Ephraim John FURNESS-25
B: 5 Oct 1852
P: Burnley, Lancashire, England
M: 29 Nov 1879 -- 6
P:
D: 21 Oct 1932
P: Teton City, Fremont, Idaho

15 Alzada Rebecca BIRD-26
B: 1 Feb 1860
P: Provo, Utah, Utah
D: 2 Feb 1935
P: Teton City, Fremont, Idaho

16 John LANGMAN CM-66
B: 6 Aug 1825
M: 26 May 1844 -- 17
D:

17 Laweza TRATHAN-67
B: 3 Mar 1822
D:

18 George CHAPMAN-843
B: 1836
M: -- 349
D: Bef 1880

19 Elizabeth Williams -844
B: 1838
D:

20 Valentine HOFFMAN-374
B: 25 Aug 1843
M: 3 Jan 1868 -- 134
D: 13 Nov 1917

21 Mary Ann MUNION-375
B: 22 Mar 1851
D: 14 Mar 1923

22 James CAMPBELL-841
B: 1844
M: 15 Dec 1867 -- 348
D:

23 Mary Treva EVERMAN-842
B: 1848
D:

24 Daniel ALLEN-442
B: 9 Dec 1804
M: 22 Jun 1847 -- 165
D: 15 Jan 1892

25 Louisa Jane BERRY-443
B: 1 Dec 1828
D: 26 Jul 1902

26 William Cooke MITCHELL-168
B: 14 Jun 1806
M: 19 Mar 1874 -- 67
D: 20 Jun 1857

27 Mary MOORE-169
B: 19 Nov 1821
D: 18 Aug 1907

28 Robert FURNESS-945
B: 28 Mar 1830
M: 16 Feb 1848 -- 391
D: 16 Nov 1894

29 Bennett LUPTON-946
B: 3 Apr 1828
D: 12 Oct 1890

30 John Pratt Kennedy BIRD-27
B:
M: 10 Mar 1886 -- 7
D: 27 Mar1886

31 Sarah Ann HOOPES-28
B: 31 Jan 1830
D: 27 Jun 1910

Prepared by
Robert R. Langman, Ph D
84 West 7500 South
Midvale, Utah
Salt Lake
Telephone 801-568-0154
Date prepared 14 Jul 2000

"A thing is important if any one thinks it important."

-The Principles of Psychology. Chap. 28

Notes are a very important part of your records. The notes you prepare may be the most important documents in your genealogy notebook. They need to be carefully prepared. They need to be organized in a uniform manner so that anyone reading them will know what to expect. All of your important information should be verified and listed, then documented and preserved. The following is a list of such information; detailed notations, references, past research efforts, present research being conducted and future research plans. All these notes will help verify the individual you are researching.

Make up research notes, enter information into data management program, then print.

Research Notes

-Make notations as research is completed

-Keep tract of your genealogy research in your notes

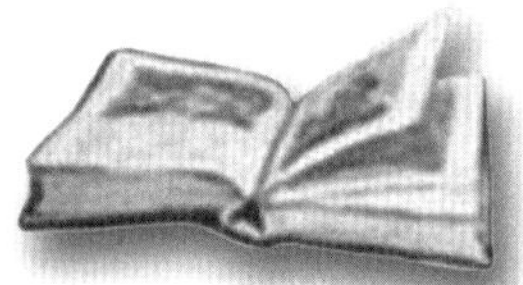

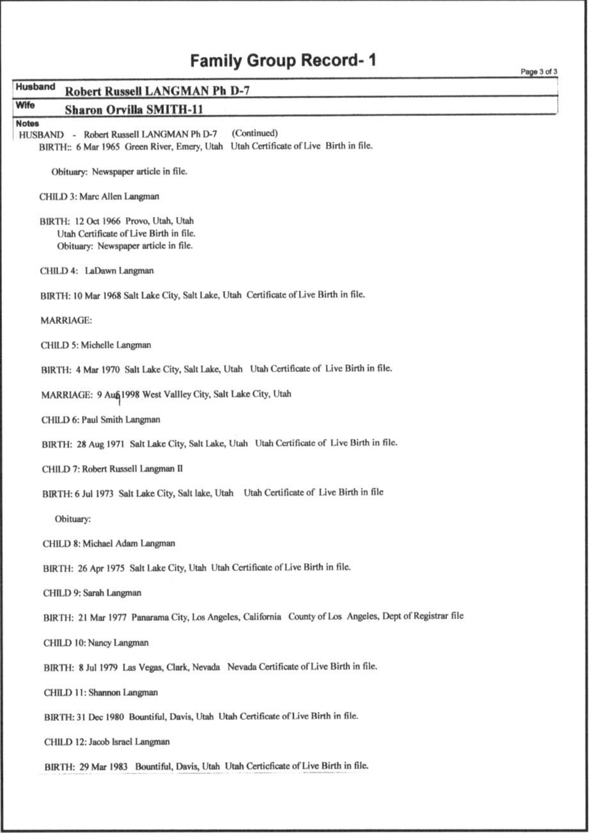

Family Group Record- 1

Page 3 of 3

Husband **Robert Russell LANGMAN Ph D-7**

Wife **Sharon Orvilla SMITH-11**

Notes

HUSBAND - Robert Russell LANGMAN Ph D-7 (Continued)

BIRTH:: 6 Mar 1965 Green River, Emery, Utah Utah Certificate of Live Birth in file.

Obituary: Newspaper article in file.

CHILD 3: Marc Allen Langman

BIRTH: 12 Oct 1966 Provo, Utah, Utah
Utah Certificate of Live Birth in file.
Obituary: Newspaper article in file.

CHILD 4: LaDawn Langman

BIRTH: 10 Mar 1968 Salt Lake City, Salt Lake, Utah Certificate of Live Birth in file.

MARRIAGE:

CHILD 5: Michelle Langman

BIRTH: 4 Mar 1970 Salt Lake City, Salt Lake, Utah Utah Certificate of Live Birth in file.

MARRIAGE: 9 Aug 1998 West Vallley City, Salt Lake City, Utah

CHILD 6: Paul Smith Langman

BIRTH: 28 Aug 1971 Salt Lake City, Salt Lake, Utah Utah Certificate of Live Birth in file.

CHILD 7: Robert Russell Langman II

BIRTH: 6 Jul 1973 Salt Lake City, Salt lake, Utah Utah Certificate of Live Birth in file

Obituary:

CHILD 8: Michael Adam Langman

BIRTH: 26 Apr 1975 Salt Lake City, Utah Utah Certificate of Live Birth in file.

CHILD 9: Sarah Langman

BIRTH: 21 Mar 1977 Panarama City, Los Angeles, California County of Los Angeles, Dept of Registrar file

CHILD 10: Nancy Langman

BIRTH: 8 Jul 1979 Las Vegas, Clark, Nevada Nevada Certificate of Live Birth in file.

CHILD 11: Shannon Langman

BIRTH: 31 Dec 1980 Bountiful, Davis, Utah Utah Certificate of Live Birth in file.

CHILD 12: Jacob Israel Langman

BIRTH: 29 Mar 1983 Bountiful, Davis, Utah Utah Certicficate of Live Birth in file.

Chapter 11 "Organize by SURNAME"

Review from Chapter 10

1. Fill in your pedigree charts as completely as possible
2. Write your notes which will tract your research

Put papers and documents into alphabetical order into Notebooks:

Assemble your papers and documents into your notebooks in alphabetical order by SURNAME.

Pedigree Chart

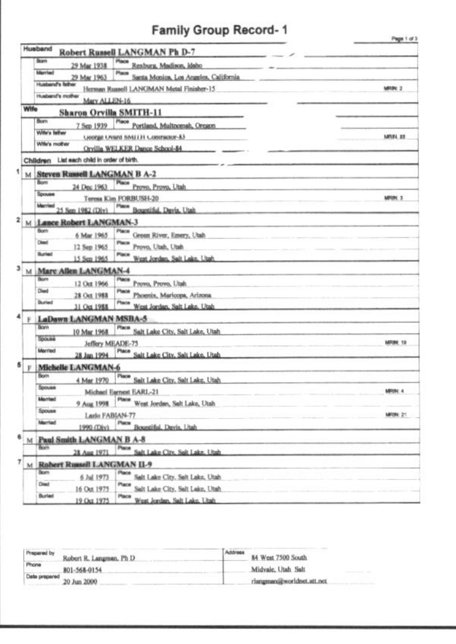

Family Group Record- 1

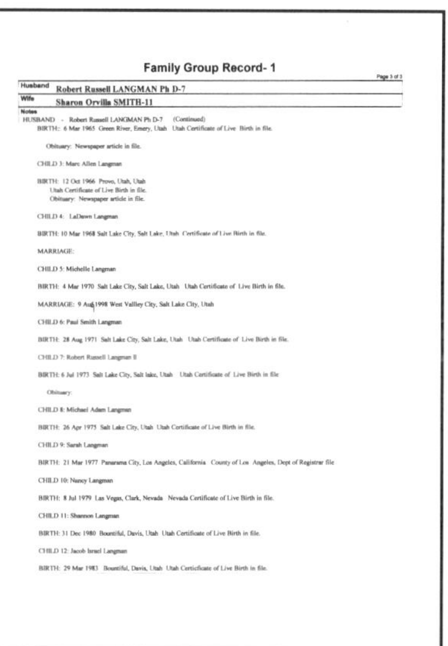

Family Group Record- 1

Use of Notebooks for Pedigree Charts, Family Group Records and Research Notes:

A copy of each 5 generation pedigree chart and extended pedigree charts, should be organized in numerical order(see Illustration on page 68). Insertable dividers with a numbered tab should be placed in front of each pedigree chart. When completed, there should be many extended pedigree charts organized in numerical order.

In the first notebook, place all your pedigree charts. Organize your pedigree charts with extensions and put them into your notebook.

Put your Family Group Records into Notebooks

The second notebook will hold your family group records, listing the name and dates of the father mother and children (see Illustration on 92 & 93). Your family group records will be organized in alphabetical order by SURNAME, given name, then by date.

Put your family group records in alphabetical order. Put them in order by SURNAME, then slide them into the Notebook.

Put Family Group Records in Alphabetical Order
by SURNAME
Then put into the Notebook

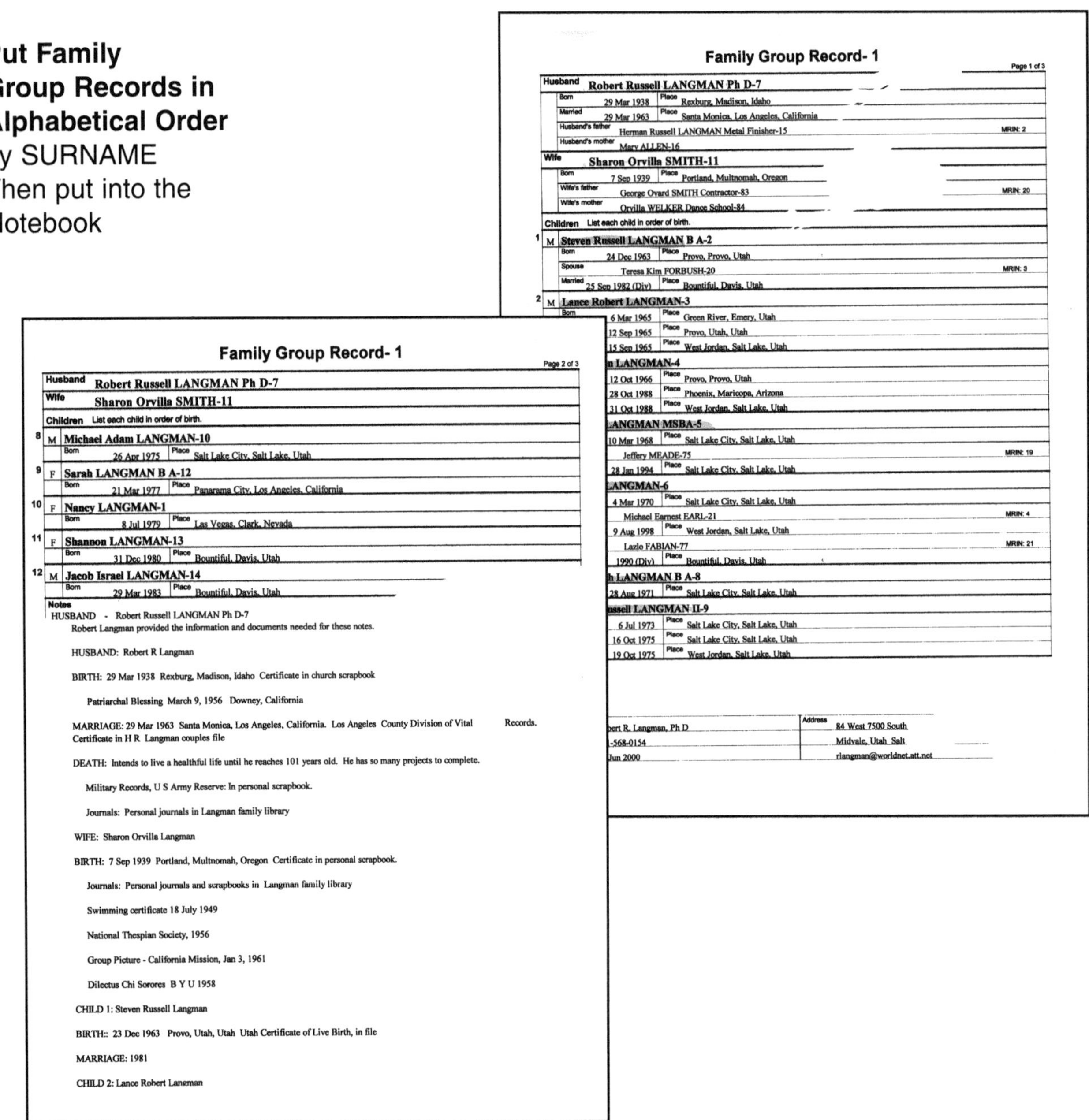

Family Group Record- 1

Page 1 of 3

Husband Robert Russell LANGMAN Ph D-7
Born 29 Mar 1938 Place Rexburg, Madison, Idaho
Married 29 Mar 1963 Place Santa Monica, Los Angeles, California
Husband's father Herman Russell LANGMAN Metal Finisher-15 MRIN: 2
Husband's mother Mary ALLEN-16

Wife Sharon Orvilla SMITH-11
Born 7 Sep 1939 Place Portland, Multnomah, Oregon
Wife's father George Ovard SMITH Contractor-83 MRIN: 20
Wife's mother Orvilla WELKER Dance School-84

Children List each child in order of birth.

1 M Steven Russell LANGMAN B A-2
Born 24 Dec 1963 Place Provo, Provo, Utah
Spouse Teresa Kim FORBUSH-20 MRIN: 3
Married 25 Sep 1982 (Div) Place Bountiful, Davis, Utah

2 M Lance Robert LANGMAN-3
Born 6 Mar 1965 Place Green River, Emery, Utah
12 Sep 1965 Place Provo, Utah, Utah
15 Sep 1965 Place West Jordan, Salt Lake, Utah

n LANGMAN-4
12 Oct 1966 Place Provo, Provo, Utah
28 Oct 1988 Place Phoenix, Maricopa, Arizona
31 Oct 1988 Place West Jordan, Salt Lake, Utah

LANGMAN MSBA-5
10 Mar 1968 Place Salt Lake City, Salt Lake, Utah
Jeffery MEADE-75 MRIN: 19
28 Jan 1994 Place Salt Lake City, Salt Lake, Utah

LANGMAN-6
4 Mar 1970 Place Salt Lake City, Salt Lake, Utah
Michael Earnest EARL-21 MRIN: 4
9 Aug 1998 Place West Jordan, Salt Lake, Utah
Lazlo FABIAN-77 MRIN: 21
1990 (Div) Place Bountiful, Davis, Utah

h LANGMAN B A-8
28 Aug 1971 Place Salt Lake City, Salt Lake, Utah

ussell LANGMAN II-9
6 Jul 1973 Place Salt Lake City, Salt Lake, Utah
16 Oct 1975 Place Salt Lake City, Salt Lake, Utah
19 Oct 1975 Place West Jordan, Salt Lake, Utah

bert R. Langman, Ph D
-568-0154
Jun 2000
Address 84 West 7500 South
Midvale, Utah Salt
rlangman@worldnet.att.net

Family Group Record- 1

Page 2 of 3

Husband Robert Russell LANGMAN Ph D-7
Wife Sharon Orvilla SMITH-11

Children List each child in order of birth.

8 M Michael Adam LANGMAN-10
Born 26 Apr 1975 Place Salt Lake City, Salt Lake, Utah

9 F Sarah LANGMAN B A-12
Born 21 Mar 1977 Place Panarama City, Los Angeles, California

10 F Nancy LANGMAN-1
Born 8 Jul 1979 Place Las Vegas, Clark, Nevada

11 F Shannon LANGMAN-13
Born 31 Dec 1980 Place Bountiful, Davis, Utah

12 M Jacob Israel LANGMAN-14
Born 29 Mar 1983 Place Bountiful, Davis, Utah

Notes
HUSBAND - Robert Russell LANGMAN Ph D-7
Robert Langman provided the information and documents needed for these notes.

HUSBAND: Robert R Langman

BIRTH: 29 Mar 1938 Rexburg, Madison, Idaho Certificate in church scrapbook

Patriarchal Blessing March 9, 1956 Downey, California

MARRIAGE: 29 Mar 1963 Santa Monica, Los Angeles, California. Los Angeles County Division of Vital Records. Certificate in H R Langman couples file

DEATH: Intends to live a healthful life until he reaches 101 years old. He has so many projects to complete.

Military Records, U S Army Reserve: In personal scrapbook.

Journals: Personal journals in Langman family library

WIFE: Sharon Orvilla Langman

BIRTH: 7 Sep 1939 Portland, Multnomah, Oregon Certificate in personal scrapbook.

Journals: Personal journals and scrapbooks in Langman family library

Swimming certificate 18 July 1949

National Thespian Society, 1956

Group Picture - California Mission, Jan 3, 1961

Dilectus Chi Sorores B Y U 1958

CHILD 1: Steven Russell Langman

BIRTH:: 23 Dec 1963 Provo, Utah, Utah Utah Certificate of Live Birth, in file

MARRIAGE: 1981

CHILD 2: Lance Robert Langman

Chapter 12 "A Place for All"

Review from Chapter 11

1. Put papers and documents in your notebook by surname
2. Put pedigree charts, family group records and notes in notebook by surname

"And beholding your order..." *-Colossians 2:5*

Put your documents and papers in the following order. If you store all of your papers and documents in order, finding your papers and documents will be easy.

Step 6:

Make 16 copies of Pedigree Charts. Highlight a parents name for each.

-A copy of the five (5) generation pedigree chart with highlighted surnames (see Illustration on page 65).

-A copy of the family group record(see Illustration on page 66 & 67).

-Research notes, printed as a separate document, not attached to family group record (see Illustration on page 68 & 69).

-Original source or primary documents, i.e., birth, marriage and death certificates

-Copies of secondary documents, i.e., census index, histories, and other family histories.

-Any number of pictures

-Awards and certificates of accomplishments

Let's get started by organizing your Notebooks:

Set aside a place to do your genealogy work. It would be nice to have a desk, chair, and telephone. (And include some peace and quiet.) Assemble all your materials, ie., documents and papers, several 2," three ring notebooks, polypropylene acid free, non-stick sheet protectors, white acid free 81/2" x 11" paper, a set of alphabetical indexes (A - Z), a set of insertable dividers with clear tabs and a set of insertable dividers with numbered tabs.

Open your "2," three ring quality notebook, assemble the following materials:

Using a polypropylene acid free, non-stick, sheet protectors for each of your papers and documents. Slide your first five-(5) generation pedigree chart into the sheet protector. Place it behind an insertable divider with numbered tabs. Place the first pedigree chart behind tab number one (1). Place tabs two (2) through seventeen (17) in your notebook. Put documents and papers behind number 2 through 17 in your notebook. There is a way to number the pedigree charts so that you are able to find your papers.

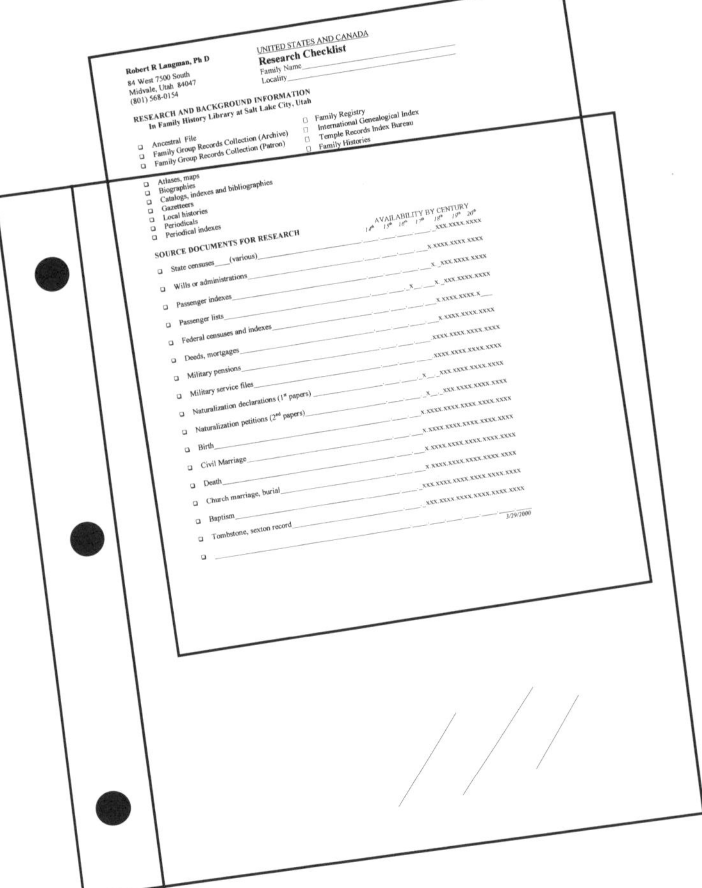

Make a Notebook of Pedigree Charts, using a next available number:

A numbering system needs to be used that will help you find the charts you need. The goal is to assign numbers to individuals as they are added to the pedigree and extended pedigree charts.

Pre-assigned number for names on your Pedigree Chart:

This system has a pre-assigned number for each individual on the pedigree chart. If a space is blank and there is no name listed on the pedigree, the space and number is reserved. Our goal is to number each individual on every pedigree chart. There is a formula that will account for every individual. A numbering system needs to be used that will help you successfully find the charts you need. The desire is to have a pre-assigned number to every ancestor whether you have a name or not. So when you eventually find that ancestor it will have logical numbers in sequence waiting to be given a name.

The next available number

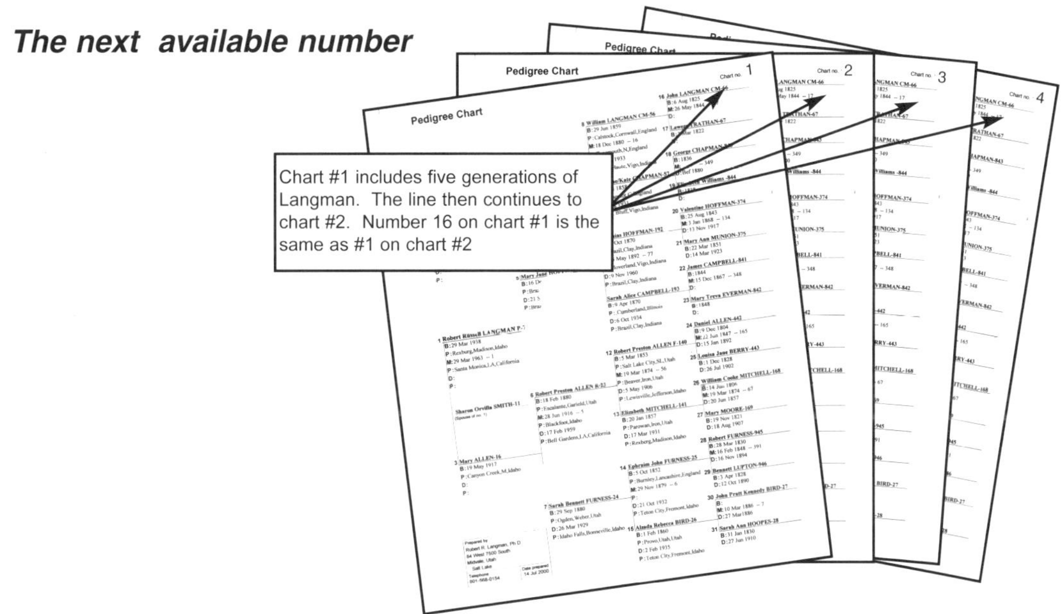

Pre-assigned numbers

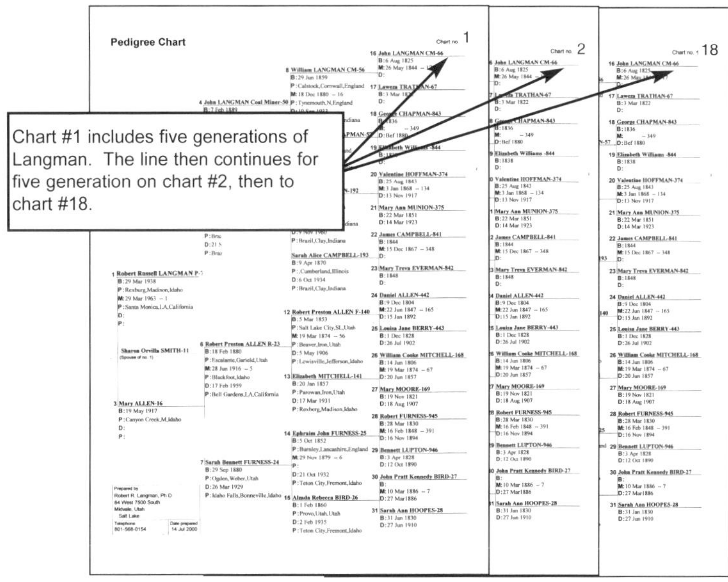

The Second Set of Notebooks will be used to store your Family Group Records:

Open Notebook # 2 and place your family group records in alphabetical order by surname, include the rest of your papers and documents.

There are two sets of insertable dividers needed for your filing system. The first set of dividers will used to put your papers in alphabetical order (A -Z). The second set of insertable dividers will have a clear vinyl tab and a colored paper insert. On the colored paper insert, print your family SURNAMES.

Then, put your family group records in alphabetical order by SURNAME. Place the family group records behind your alphabetized dividers. Keep all of your family group records that have the same SURNAME together. Then organize your family group records by given name.

Step 7:

Place your Pedigree Chart, Family Group Records, & Notes in a notebook

Place insertable dividers with clear vinyl tab and a colored paper insert into Notebook.

The position and color of the vinyl tab will indicate which ancestral line you are following:

> **Step 8:**
>
> **Assemble papers in alphabetical note books. Pedigree, Family Group Records, Notes, and Papers**

The position and color of the tab will help find the family ancestor. When you put away a file, the position and color of the tab will help locate an ancestor more effectively. For example, you will clearly identify your husband's father because it will be the in the first position and have a blue tab.

Research Notes:

Behind the family group records put a copy of the research notes. All research notes should be set up in a uniform and consistent manner. When each set of notes is uniform and consistent, the reader is comfortable with the repetition and the reader knows what to expect and knows how to find information quickly. List all the references and notations that verify the information collected (this should include research that brought no results) (see Illustration on page 68 & 69).

The Rest of the Documents:

The easiest way to find your documents is to put them away in a uniform manner. Original source documents, i.e., birth, marriage and death certificates are placed behind the notes.

Copies of secondary documents, i.e., census index, histories, and other genealogies are placed behind source documents. Copies of life stories are placed behind secondary documents, along with any number of pictures, awards, certificates of accomplishments and any thing else of importance.

Chapter 13 "Tools To Help You Organize"

Review from Chapter 12

1. Get started in organizing your notebooks
2. Assemble your materials and put into notebooks
3. Use a numbering system to organize your pedigree charts
4. Place family group records in alphabetical order

It is important for a genealogy researcher to use tools to help you get organized.

There is a tool for every job. In order to make the job more efficient it is important to use the right tool. Tools to help you get organized make the work more efficient. Please look over the following tools and review the definition for use.

Step 9:

Research packet To Do List, Research Checklist, Research Log, Map, Time Line

Tools to Help You get Organized Go into Notebook

-To Do List
-Research Checklist
-Research Log
-Time Line
-Maps

Geneology Research

To Do List

Name to research ____________

Date Started ____________

1.
2.
3.
4.
5.
6.
7.
8.
9.
10.

Time Line

Most Ancient Historical Events

Most Recent Historical Events

Dates____________________

Most Ancient Personal History

Most Recent Personal History

By: Robert R Langman, Ph D

Robert R Langman, Ph D
84 West 7500 South
Midvale, Utah 84047
(801)568-0154

UNITED STATES
Research Checklist
Family Name____________________
Locality____________________

SOURCE DOCUMENTS FOR RESEARCH

HOME

- ❑ Albums, Photographs
- ❑ Diaries, Journals
- ❑ Family Bible and Letters
- ☐ Internet
- ☐ Interviews
- ☐ Traditions

TOWN RECORDS

- ❑ Cemetery Records
- ❑ City or County Records
- ❑ Funeral Home Records
- ☐ Histories
- ☐ Newspaper Files
- ☐ Public School Records

COUNTY RECORDS

- ❑ Administration of Estates
- ❑ Civil & Criminal Court Records
- ❑ County Historical Society
- ❑ Deeds & Mortgages
- ❑ Militia Records
- ☐ Naturalization Tax and Voter's Lists
- ☐ Probate, Wills, Guardianships
- ☐ Sheriff's Sales
- ☐ Tax and Voter's Lists
- ☐ Vital Records: Birth/Marriage/Death

STATE RECORDS

- ❑ Accounts & Journals
- ❑ Homestead & Donation Land Claims
- ❑ Land Grants
- ❑ State Archives
- ☐ State Census
- ☐ State Historical Society
- ☐ Supreme & Appellate Court Records
- ☐ Vital Records

NATIONAL RECORDS

- ❑ Bounty Land Records
- ❑ Census (1790-1920)
- ❑ Circuit Court of Appeals
- ❑ District & Supreme Court Records
- ❑ Immigration Records
- ❑ Military Land Grants & Military Records
- ❑ Mortality Schedules - Census years
- ☐ National Archives
- ☐ National Historical Society
- ☐ Passenger Lists
- ☐ Pay Vouchers and Pension Records
- ☐ Public and Private Land Claims
- ☐ Vital Registration

LIBRARIES

- ❑ Biographical Compendia
- ❑ C D Pro-Phone
- ❑ Cemetery Records
- ❑ Church Records & Histories
- ❑ D A R Lineage Books
- ❑ D A R Patriot Index
- ☐ Directories to funeral homes&cemeteries
- ☐ Genealogies
- ☐ Interlibrary Loan
- ☐ Newspapers on Microfilm
- ☐ Obituary Collections and Indexes
- ☐ Printed and Manuscript Histories

Robert R Langman, Ph D
84 West 7500 South
Midvale, Utah 84047
(801) 568-0154

UNITED STATES AND CANADA
Research Checklist
Family Name____________________
Locality____________________

RESEARCH AND BACKGROUND INFORMATION
In Family History Library at Salt Lake City, Utah

- ❑ Ancestral File
- ❑ Family Group Records Collection (Archive)
- ❑ Family Group Records Collection (Patron)
- ☐ Family Registry
- ☐ International Genealogical Index
- ☐ Temple Records Index Bureau
- ☐ Family Histories

- ❑ Atlases, maps
- ❑ Biographies
- ❑ Catalogs, indexes and bibliographies
- ❑ Gazetteers
- ❑ Local histories
- ❑ Periodicals
- ❑ Periodical indexes

SOURCE DOCUMENTS FOR RESEARCH — AVAILABILITY BY CENTURY
14th 15th 16th 17th 18th 19th 20th

- ❑ State censuses____(various)________ .____.____.____.____._XXX.XXXX.XXXX
- ❑ Wills or administrations________ .____.____.____.___X.XXXX.XXXX.XXXX
- ❑ Passenger indexes________ .____.____.____.___X._XXX.XXXX.XXXX
- ❑ Passenger lists________ .____.____._X__.___X._XXX.XXXX.XXXX
- ❑ Federal censuses and indexes________ .____.____.____.___X.XXXX.XXXX.X___
- ❑ Deeds, mortgages________ .____.____.____.___X.XXXX.XXXX.XXXX
- ❑ Military pensions________ .____.____.____.XXXX.XXXX.XXXX.XXXX
- ❑ Military service files________ .____.____.____.XXXX.XXXX.XXXX.XXXX
- ❑ Naturalization declarations (1st papers) ________ .____.____._X__._XXX.XXXX.XXXX.XXXX
- ❑ Naturalization petitions (2nd papers)________ .____.____._X__._XXX.XXXX.XXXX.XXXX
- ❑ Birth________ .____.___X.XXXX.XXXX.XXXX.XXXX.XXXX
- ❑ Civil Marriage________ .____.___X.XXXX.XXXX.XXXX.XXXX.XXXX
- ❑ Death________ .____.___X.XXXX.XXXX.XXXX.XXXX.XXXX
- ❑ Church marriage, burial________ .____.___X.XXXX.XXXX.XXXX.XXXX.XXXX
- ❑ Baptism________ .____._XXX.XXXX.XXXX.XXXX.XXXX.XXXX
- ❑ Tombstone, sexton record________ .____._XXX.XXXX.XXXX.XXXX.XXXX.XXXX
- ❑ ________ .____.____.____.____.____.____.____

3/29/2000

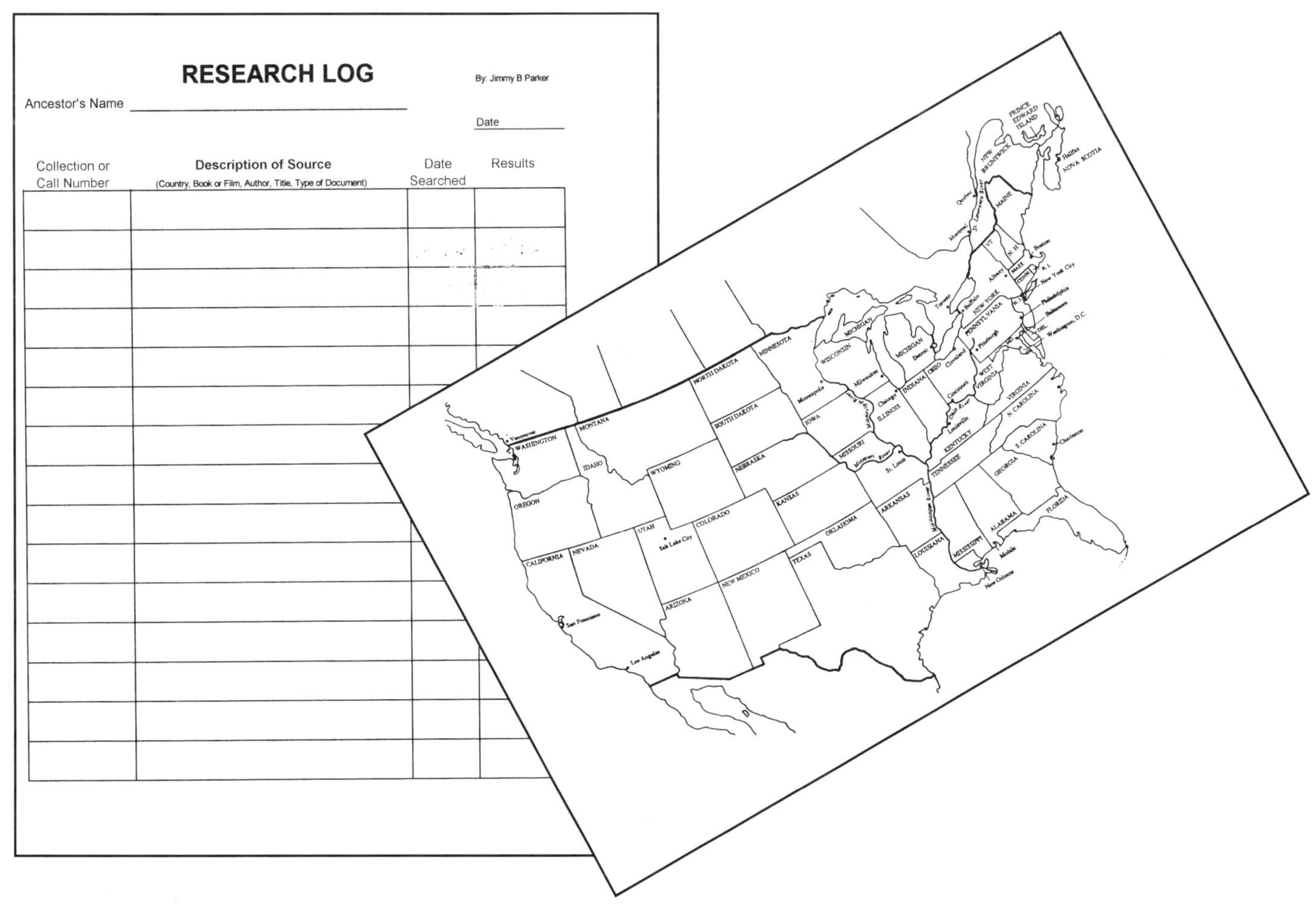

RESEARCH LOG

By: Jimmy B Parker

Ancestor's Name ____________________

Date ________

Collection or Call Number	Description of Source (Country, Book or Film, Author, Title, Type of Document)	Date Searched	Results

"Windshield Watching in Salt Lake City"

Long before the 2002 Winter Olympics in Utah, the streets and freeways were all under constructions in preparation for this once in a life time event. Every road had rocks and debris on it, which had fallen from the construction trucks. As Salt Lakers drove the streets everyday, the tires on the cars in front of them would throw rocks into the air. Some of the rocks would strike the windshields of cars. At the end of each day, Salt Lakers would carefully check their windshields for cracks and pit marks. They wanted to know the status of their cars' windshields.

All genealogy researchers need to check the status of their research efforts.

Tools to help you get organized assist genealogists on the status of their research efforts:

1 - The "To Do List" includes notations made of future research to be performed. This can be filled out at any time and at any place, especially when ideas come to mind (See illustration on page 70).

2 -The Research Checklist is a list of all types of documents and paper sources. This checklist is to be used in order to help find the needed genealogy information that will help prove the existence of an individual. When a document has been researched, check off each item as it was searched. This is done to avoid research duplication. The list will also be a reminder of research that still needs to be done. Also, included on the checklist is *Availability by Century Chart.* The purpose for this chart is to alert the researcher of the dates the document actually existed.(See illustration on pages 71 & 72).

3 - The Research Log is a record of past research already completed with references and sources. This is to be used to take research notes while in the library. This log can be put into your notes, the SURNAME file or a separate file for your logs (See illustration on page 74).

4 - Maps of the area being researched should be included, (Example, country, state, county, township or cities) (see illustration on page 75).

5 - The Time Line is a research tool that will help locate information. This is to be filled out to compare the individual events with historical events. This comparison should bring forth your date and place clues for investigation (See illustration on page 73).

Step 10:

Place research aids and helps in filing system

When the Notebook is Completed This Is What They should Look Like This:

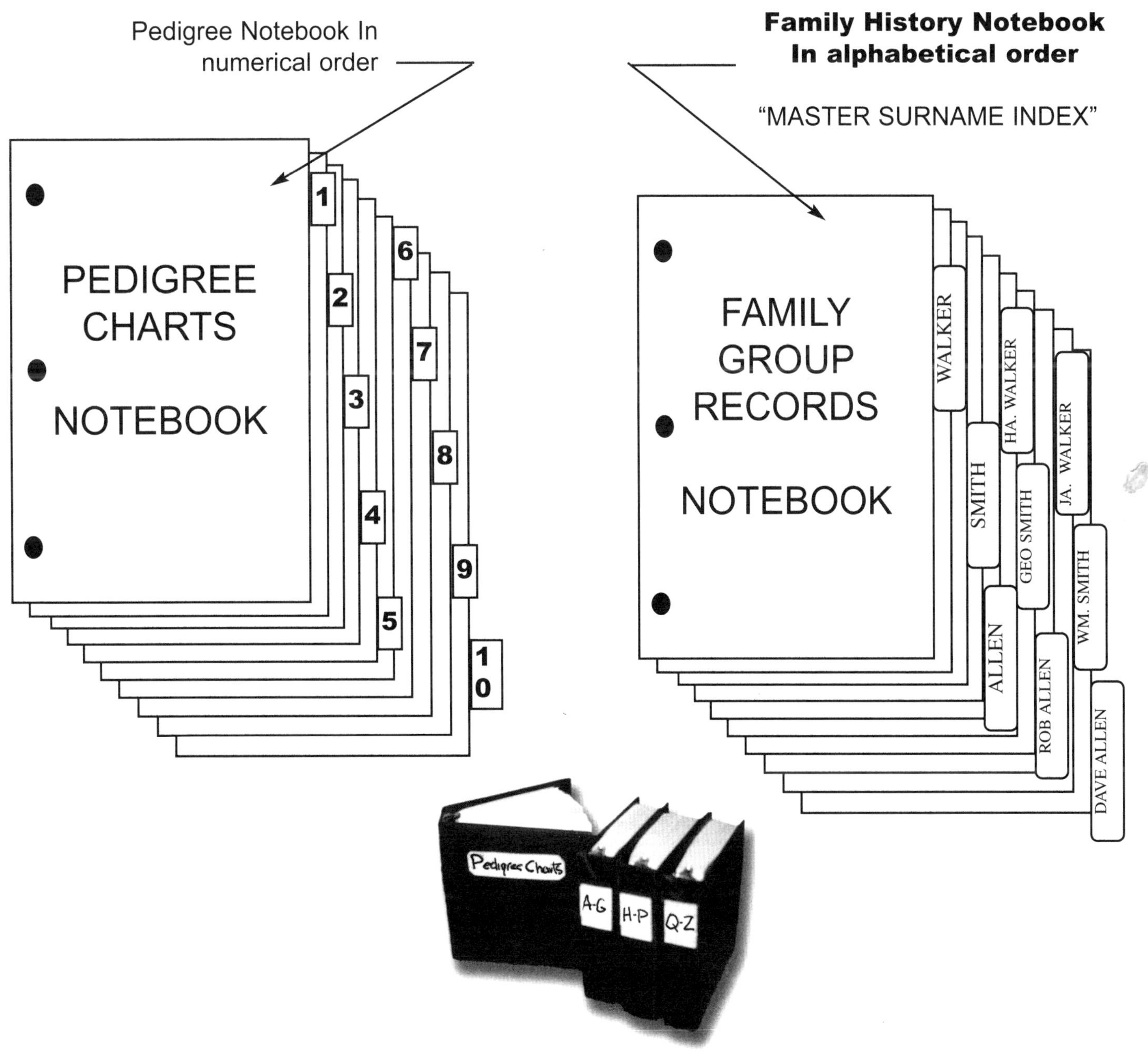

Chapter 14 Reviewing the Ten Steps For Your Notebooks

Review from Chapter 13

1. You use tools to help organize your genealogy work
2. The rule is to put your papers away so that they can be found

In summary, there are ten steps to set up notebook filing system:

Organization will inspire a genealogy researcher to continue their work. It is true that when we organize our genealogy properly, we will continue to maintain your interest and the research will thrive. We will be "doers" of genealogy rather than just "talkers." Organizing your genealogy system will allow you to find any document or paper quickly.

1. - Put all loose papers and documents into one place, then sort into piles by SURNAME.

2.- Two sets of notebooks will be used to file your genealogy. The first will notebook will be used to place your pedigree charts in numerical order. The second will be used to place your family group sheets.

3.- Two sets of insertable dividers are needed. The first is a set of numerical insertable dividers that are used to organize your pedigree charts. The second is a set of insertable dividers to be used to organize your family group records in alphabetical (A through Z) order.

4.- The alphabetical insertable dividers have five tabs down the right side of the notebook. The position of the tab will identify your family lines. When you add color to each family line then position and color identify your four family lines by SURNAME.

5.- Print your pedigree charts and family group records and notes from your computer data management program (if you prefer to type or write by hand that is good).

6.- Make sixteen 16 copies of the pedigree charts and highlight each couple surname on the chart, one different couple per page.

7.- Place your pedigree, family group records and notes, into your alphabetized notebooks.

8.- Assembled your documents and place them into your notebook.

You place them the following order: Pedigree Chart, Family Group Records, Notes, primary and secondary documents.

9.- Prepare your research packet and place into notebook behind your notes, i.e., To Do List, Research Checklist, Research Log, Map and Time Line.

10. - Set up a section in the filing system for research aids and helps.

When this all completed, you will be able to locate any paper within "30 Seconds."

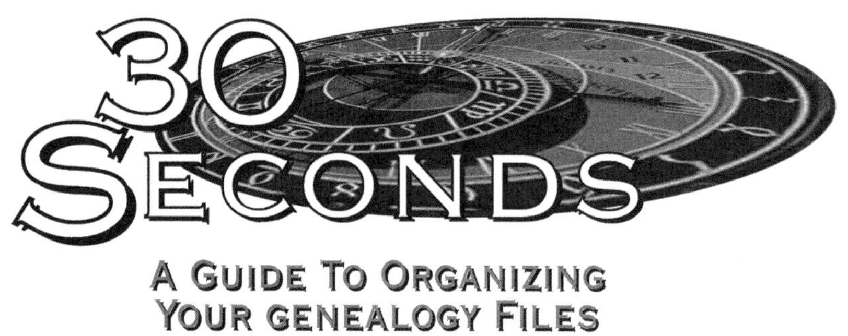

Part 3: In Summary

Chapter 15 *Principles To Live By*

We have discovered some important principles through he years of research experience that will make you life as a researcher much easier. We want to share them with you because we don't want you to have to go through as much pain as we have in order to learn all these principles.

Some of these principles may seem pretty simple. Some you may have thought of yourself and may already be applying them to your research. But, perhaps some of them may be new to you.

We know that if you consistently apply these principles, they will make everything else in you filing and retrieving easier.

If you apply nothing else from this book, try to apply the principles i this summary. They are the essence of good filing retrieving of your papers.

Simplify
However you do it, do it simply. Complicated systems are hard to use time-consuming.

Your filing system should be simple enough so that any genealogist or family member would be able to find any document quickly and easily. Consider what would happen to your genealogy if you should suddenly die. Some day, someone will inherit your genealogy work. Will they want to continue your work? Or will they become so frustrated with your files that they will simply get rid of them?

For ease of filing , record you research results about one SURNAME per page. When you record several SURNAMES in your research on one page, it becomes difficult to file your papers.

Standardize
Use a standard size paper (8.5x11) for all your note-taking. Small-sized paper notes get misplaced, crushed in a file folder or lost.

Use whit acid free paper for long life. Colored paper fades over a short time. High-acid content in paper discolors and gets brittle quickly.

Record your researchings accurately and consistently. Give as much attention to recording searches which produce negative result, as you do those that produce positive results. If you do not record negative searches, you will repeat them until you do.

Record you research results completely enough that you or anyone else seeing you notes could go back to the sources of the information. This means some minimum standards of documentation need to be established.

However you do, be consistent. Doing things the some way promotes accuracy.

Adapt
Decide on the type of filing system you want to use, Then get started. Be sure you are comfortable with your system.

Your filing system should meet the needs of the locality of you research. Patronymics or other situation may require an adjustment in your filing system.

Order
Bringing order to your filing system will encourage further research efforts. Knowing where to find papers or references in your filing system will allow you to succeed.

Genealogy research is fun, exciting and rewarding. But the sheer volume of information available on our families is usaully enough that it can easily overwhelm and discourage us if we don't have an organized system in place to handle it. And if we are disorganized, we not only can become discouraged, but we can certainl,y overwhelm family members that may inherit our work after we're gone.

- Jimmy Parker

Addendum

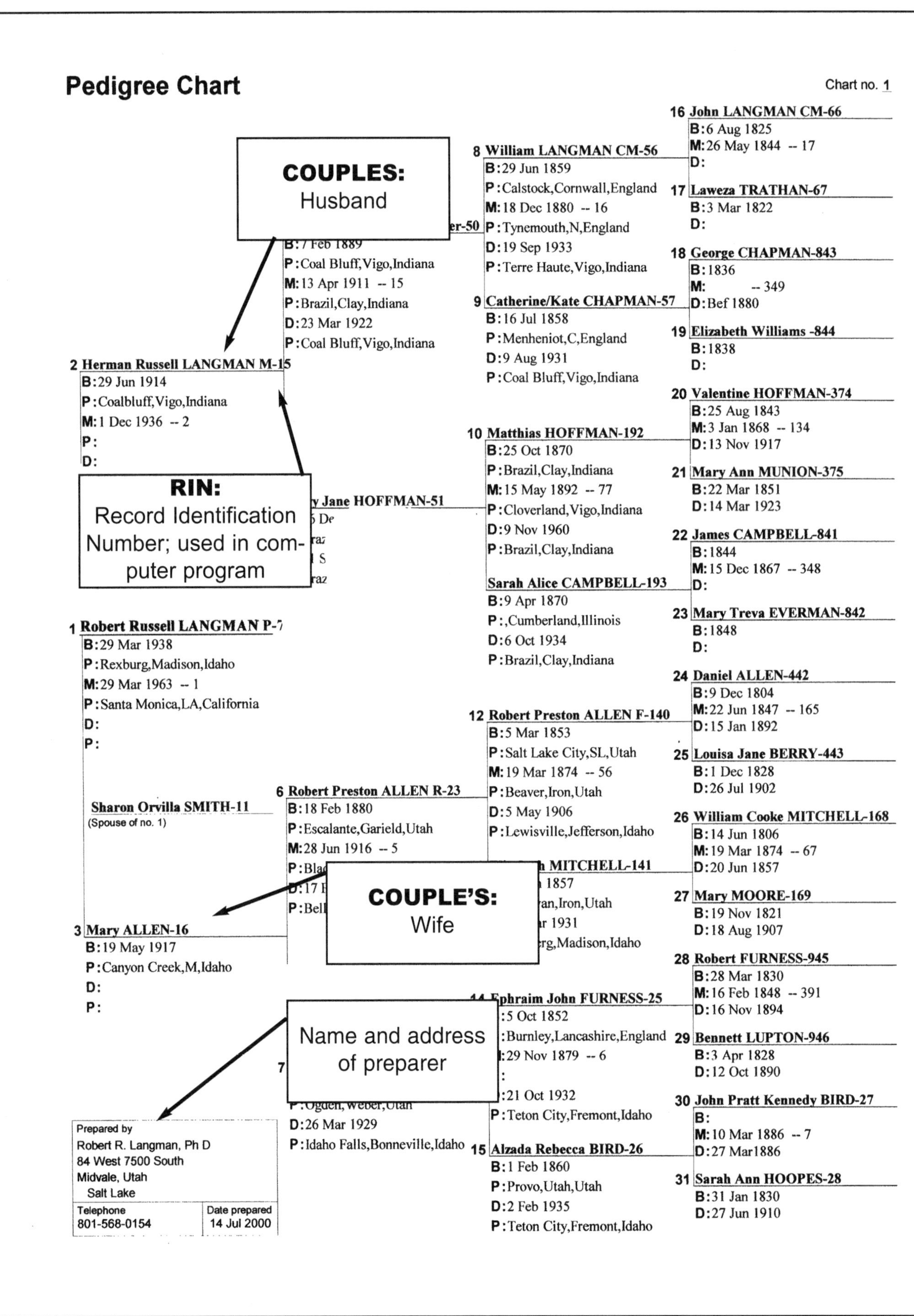
Pedigree Chart
Chart no. 1
COUPLES:
Husband
RIN:
Record Identification Number; used in computer program
COUPLE'S:
Wife
Name and address of preparer
16 John LANGMAN CM-66
B:6 Aug 1825
M:26 May 1844 -- 17
D:
17 Laweza TRATHAN-67
B:3 Mar 1822
D:
8 William LANGMAN CM-56
B:29 Jun 1859
P:Calstock,Cornwall,England
M:18 Dec 1880 -- 16
P:Tynemouth,N,England
D:19 Sep 1933
P:Terre Haute,Vigo,Indiana
18 George CHAPMAN-843
B:1836
M: -- 349
D:Bef 1880
9 Catherine/Kate CHAPMAN-57
B:16 Jul 1858
P:Menheniot,C,England
D:9 Aug 1931
P:Coal Bluff,Vigo,Indiana
19 Elizabeth Williams -844
B:1838
D:
P:Coal Bluff,Vigo,Indiana
M:13 Apr 1911 -- 15
P:Brazil,Clay,Indiana
D:23 Mar 1922
P:Coal Bluff,Vigo,Indiana
2 Herman Russell LANGMAN M-15
B:29 Jun 1914
P:Coalbluff,Vigo,Indiana
M:1 Dec 1936 -- 2
P:
D:
20 Valentine HOFFMAN-374
B:25 Aug 1843
M:3 Jan 1868 -- 134
D:13 Nov 1917
10 Matthias HOFFMAN-192
B:25 Oct 1870
P:Brazil,Clay,Indiana
M:15 May 1892 -- 77
P:Cloverland,Vigo,Indiana
D:9 Nov 1960
P:Brazil,Clay,Indiana
21 Mary Ann MUNION-375
B:22 Mar 1851
D:14 Mar 1923
22 James CAMPBELL-841
B:1844
M:15 Dec 1867 -- 348
D:
Sarah Alice CAMPBELL-193
B:9 Apr 1870
P:,Cumberland,Illinois
D:6 Oct 1934
P:Brazil,Clay,Indiana
23 Mary Treva EVERMAN-842
B:1848
D:
1 Robert Russell LANGMAN P-7
B:29 Mar 1938
P:Rexburg,Madison,Idaho
M:29 Mar 1963 -- 1
P:Santa Monica,LA,California
D:
P:
24 Daniel ALLEN-442
B:9 Dec 1804
M:22 Jun 1847 -- 165
D:15 Jan 1892
12 Robert Preston ALLEN F-140
B:5 Mar 1853
P:Salt Lake City,SL,Utah
M:19 Mar 1874 -- 56
P:Beaver,Iron,Utah
D:5 May 1906
P:Lewisville,Jefferson,Idaho
25 Louisa Jane BERRY-443
B:1 Dec 1828
D:26 Jul 1902
Sharon Orvilla SMITH-11
(Spouse of no. 1)
6 Robert Preston ALLEN R-23
B:18 Feb 1880
P:Escalante,Garield,Utah
M:28 Jun 1916 -- 5
26 William Cooke MITCHELL-168
B:14 Jun 1806
M:19 Mar 1874 -- 67
D:20 Jun 1857
27 Mary MOORE-169
B:19 Nov 1821
D:18 Aug 1907
3 Mary ALLEN-16
B:19 May 1917
P:Canyon Creek,M,Idaho
D:
P:
28 Robert FURNESS-945
B:28 Mar 1830
M:16 Feb 1848 -- 391
D:16 Nov 1894
29 Bennett LUPTON-946
B:3 Apr 1828
D:12 Oct 1890
30 John Pratt Kennedy BIRD-27
B:
M:10 Mar 1886 -- 7
D:27 Mar1886
15 Alzada Rebecca BIRD-26
B:1 Feb 1860
P:Provo,Utah,Utah
D:2 Feb 1935
P:Teton City,Fremont,Idaho
31 Sarah Ann HOOPES-28
B:31 Jan 1830
D:27 Jun 1910
D:26 Mar 1929
P:Idaho Falls,Bonneville,Idaho
P:Teton City,Fremont,Idaho
Prepared by
Robert R. Langman, Ph D
84 West 7500 South
Midvale, Utah
Salt Lake
Telephone
801-568-0154
Date prepared
14 Jul 2000

Family Group Record- 1

Husband **Robert Russell LANGMAN Ph D-7**

Born	29 Mar 1938	Place	Rexburg, Madison, Idaho
Married	29 Mar 1963	Place	Santa Monica, Los Angeles, California
Husband's father	Herman Russell LANGMAN Metal Finisher-1[illegible]		MRIN: 2
Husband's mother	Mary ALLEN-16		

Wife **Sharon Orvilla SMITH-11**

Born	7 Sep 1939	Place	Portland, Multnomah, Oregon
Wife's father	George Ovard SMITH Contractor-83		MRIN: 20
Wife's mother	Orvilla WELKER Dance School-84		

Children List each child in order of birth.

1 M **Steven Russell LANGMAN B A-2**

Born	24 Dec 1963	Place	Provo, Provo, Utah
Spouse	Teresa Kim FORBUSH-20		MRIN: 3
Married	25 Sep 1982 (Div)	Place	Bountiful, Davis, Utah

2 M **Lance Robert LANGMAN-3**

Born	6 Mar 1965	Place	Green River, Emery, Utah
Died	12 Sep 1965	Place	Provo, Utah, Utah
Buried	15 Sep 1965	Place	West Jordan, Salt Lake, Utah

3 M **Marc Allen LANGMAN-4**

Born	12 Oct 1966	Place	Provo, Provo, Utah
Died	28 Oct 1988	Place	Phoenix, Maricopa, Arizona
Buried	31 Oct 1988	Place	West Jordan, Salt Lake, Utah

4 F **LaDawn LANGMAN MSBA-5**

Born	10 Mar 1968	Place	Salt Lake City, Salt Lake, Utah
Spouse	Jeffery MEADE-75		MRIN: 19
Married	28 Jan 1994	Place	Salt Lake City, Salt Lake, Utah

5 F **Michelle LANGMAN-6**

Born	4 Mar 1970	Place	Salt Lake City, Salt Lake, Utah
Spouse	Michael Earnest EARL-21		MRIN: 4
Married	9 Aug 1998	Place	West Jordan, Salt Lake, Utah
Spouse	Lazlo FABIAN-77		MRIN: 21
Married	1990 (Div)	Place	Bountiful, Davis, Utah

6 M **Paul Smith LANGMAN B A-8**

Born	28 Aug 1971	Place	Salt Lake City, Salt Lake, Utah

7 M **Robert Russell LANGMAN II-9**

Born	6 Jul 1973
Died	16 Oct 1975
Buried	19 Oct 1975

Prepared by	Robert R. Langman, Ph D	Address	84 West 7500 South
Phone	801-568-0154		Midvale, Utah Salt
Date prepared	20 Jun 2000		rlangman@worldnet.att.net

COUPLE'S: Husband and wife

RIN: Record Identification Number; used in computer program

Name and address of preparer

Family Group Record- 1

Husband	**Robert Russell LANGMAN Ph D-7**		
Wife	**Sharon Orvilla SMITH-11**		
Children List each child in order of birth.			
8 M	**Michael Adam LANGMAN-10**		
	Born 26 Apr 1975	Place	Salt Lake City, Salt Lake, Utah
9 F	**Sarah LANGMAN B A-12**		
	Born 21 Mar 1977	Place	Panarama City, Los Angeles, California
10 F	**Nancy LANGMAN-1**		
	Born 8 Jul 1979	Place	Las Vegas, Clark, Nevada
11 F	**Shannon LANGMAN-13**		
	Born 31 Dec 1980	Place	Bountiful, Davis, Utah
12 M	**Jacob Israel LANGMAN-14**		
	Born 29 Mar 1983	Place	Bountiful, Davis, Utah

Notes

HUSBAND - Robert Russell LANGMAN Ph D-7

Robert Langman provided the information and documents needed for these notes.

HUSBAND: Robert R Langman

BIRTH: 29 Mar 1938 Rexburg, Madison, Idaho Certificate in church scrapbook

Patriarchal Blessing March 9, 1956 Downey, California

MARRIAGE: 29 Mar 1963 Santa Monica, Los Angeles, California. Los Angeles County Division of Vital Records. Certificate in H R Langman couples file

DEATH: Intends to live a healthful life until he reaches 101 years old. He has so many projects to complete.

Military Records, U S Army Reserve: In personal scrapbook.

Journals: Personal journals in Langman family library

WIFE: Sharon Orvilla Langman

BIRTH: 7 Sep 1939 Portland, Multnomah, Oregon Certificate in personal scrapbook.

Journals: Personal journals and scrapbooks in Langman family library

Swimming certificate 18 July 1949

National Thespian Society, 1956

Group Picture - California Mission, Jan 3, 1961

Dilectus Chi Sorores B Y U 1958

CHILD 1: Steven Russell Langman

BIRTH:: 23 Dec 1963 Provo, Utah, Utah Utah Certificate of Live Birth, in file

MARRIAGE: 1981

CHILD 2: Lance Robert Langman

Family Group Record- 1

Husband **Robert Russell LANGMAN Ph D-7**

Wife **Sharon Orvilla SMITH-11**

Notes

HUSBAND - Robert Russell LANGMAN Ph D-7 (Continued)

BIRTH:: 6 Mar 1965 Green River, Emery, Utah Utah Certificate of Live Birth in file.

Obituary: Newspaper article in file.

CHILD 3: Marc Allen Langman

BIRTH: 12 Oct 1966 Provo, Utah, Utah
Utah Certificate of Live Birth in file.
Obituary: Newspaper article in file.

CHILD 4: LaDawn Langman

BIRTH: 10 Mar 1968 Salt Lake City, Salt Lake, Utah Certificate of Live Birth in file.

MARRIAGE:

CHILD 5: Michelle Langman

BIRTH: 4 Mar 1970 Salt Lake City, Salt Lake, Utah Utah Certificate of Live Birth in file.

MARRIAGE: 9 Aug 1998 West Vallley City, Salt Lake City, Utah

CHILD 6: Paul Smith Langman

BIRTH: 28 Aug 1971 Salt Lake City, Salt Lake, Utah Utah Certificate of Live Birth in file.

CHILD 7: Robert Russell Langman II

BIRTH: 6 Jul 1973 Salt Lake City, Salt lake, Utah Utah Certificate of Live Birth in file

Obituary:

CHILD 8: Michael Adam Langman

BIRTH: 26 Apr 1975 Salt Lake City, Utah Utah Certificate of Live Birth in file.

CHILD 9: Sarah Langman

BIRTH: 21 Mar 1977 Panarama City, Los Angeles, California County of Los Angeles, Dept of Registrar file

CHILD 10: Nancy Langman

BIRTH: 8 Jul 1979 Las Vegas, Clark, Nevada Nevada Certificate of Live Birth in file.

CHILD 11: Shannon Langman

BIRTH: 31 Dec 1980 Bountiful, Davis, Utah Utah Certificate of Live Birth in file.

CHILD 12: Jacob Israel Langman

BIRTH: 29 Mar 1983 Bountiful, Davis, Utah Utah Certicficate of Live Birth in file.

NOTES:
Husband, Wife,
Children & Sources

Family Group Record- 1

Husband Robert Russell LANGMAN Ph D-7

Wife Sharon Orvilla SMITH-11

Notes

HUSBAND - Robert Russell LANGMAN Ph D-7 (Continued)

BIRTH:: 6 Mar 1965 Green River, Emery, Utah Utah Certificate of Live Birth in file.

Obituary: Newspaper article in file.

CHILD 3: Marc Allen Langman

BIRTH: 12 Oct 1966 Provo, Utah, Utah
Utah Certificate of Live Birth in file.
Obituary: Newspaper article in file.

CHILD 4: LaDawn Langman

BIRTH: 10 Mar 1968 Salt Lake City, Salt Lake, Utah Certificate of Live Birth in file.

MARRIAGE:

CHILD 5: Michelle Langman

BIRTH: 4 Mar 1970 Salt Lake City, Salt Lake, Utah Utah Certificate of Live Birth in file.

MARRIAGE: 9 Aug 1998 West Vallley City, Salt Lake City, Utah

CHILD 6: Paul Smith Langman

BIRTH: 28 Aug 1971 Salt Lake City, Salt Lake, Utah Utah Certificate of Live Birth in file.

CHILD 7: Robert Russell Langman II

BIRTH: 6 Jul 1973 Salt Lake City, Salt lake, Utah Utah Certificate of Live Birth in file

Obituary:

CHILD 8: Michael Adam Langman

BIRTH: 26 Apr 1975 Salt Lake City, Utah Utah Certificate of Live Birth in file.

CHILD 9: Sarah Langman

BIRTH: 21 Mar 1977 Panarama City, Los Angeles, California County of Los Angeles, Dept of Registrar file

CHILD 10: Nancy Langman

BIRTH: 8 Jul 1979 Las Vegas, Clark, Nevada Nevada Certificate of Live Birth in file.

CHILD 11: Shannon Langman

BIRTH: 31 Dec 1980 Bountiful, Davis, Utah Utah Certificate of Live Birth in file.

CHILD 12: Jacob Israel Langman

BIRTH: 29 Mar 1983 Bountiful, Davis, Utah Utah Certicficate of Live Birth in file.

Geneology Research

To Do List

Name to research ______________________

Date Started ______________

1.

2.

3.

4.

5.

6.

7.

8.

9.

10.

11.

12.

13.

14.

15.

TO DO:
This is where you list all of the current research items that you are going to do immediately. To be done in order of importance.

Robert R Langman, Ph D
84 West 7500 South
Midvale, Utah 84047
(801) 568-0154

UNITED STATES AND CANADA

Research Checklist

Family Name____________________
Locality____________________

RESEARCH AND BACKGROUND INFORMATION
In Family History Library at Salt Lake City, Utah

- ❑ Ancestral File
- ❑ Family Group Records Collection (Archive)
- ❑ Family Group Records Collection (Patron)
- ☐ Family Registry
- ☐ International Genealogical Index
- ☐ Temple Records Index Bureau
- ☐ Family Histories

- ❑ Atlases, maps
- ❑ Biographies
- ❑ Catalogs, indexes and bibliographies
- ❑ Gazetteers
- ❑ Local histories
- ❑ Periodicals
- ❑ Periodical indexes

RESEARCH:
These are research sources found in the Salt Lake City Utah Family History Library

SOURCE DOCUMENTS FOR RESEARCH

AVAILABILITY BY CENTURY
14th 15th 16th 17th 18th 19th 20th

- ❑ State censuses____(various)__________ .____.____.____.____._XXX.XXXX.XXXX
- ❑ Wills or administrations__________ .____.____.____X.XXXX.XXXX.XXXX
- ❑ Passenger indexes__________ .____.____.____.X._XXX.XXXX.XXXX
- ❑ Passenger lists__________ .____
- ❑ Federal censuses and indexes__________ .____
- ❑ Deeds, mortgages__________ .____
- ❑ Military pensions__________ .____
- ❑ Military service files__________ .____.____.____
- ❑ Naturalization declarations (1st papers)__________ .____.____._X__._XXX.XXXX.XXXX.XXXX
- ❑ Naturalization petitions (2nd papers)__________ .____.____._X__._XXX.XXXX.XXXX.XXXX
- ❑ Birth__________ .____.___X.XXXX.XXXX.XXXX.XXXX.XXXX
- ❑ Civil Marriage__________ .____.___X.XXXX.XXXX.XXXX.XXXX.XXXX
- ❑ Death__________ .____.___X.XXXX.XXXX.XXXX.XXXX.XXXX
- __________ .____.___X.XXXX.XXXX.XXXX.XXXX.XXXX
- __________ .____._XXX.XXXX.XXXX.XXXX.XXXX.XXXX
- __________ .____._XXX.XXXX.XXXX.XXXX.XXXX.XXXX
- ❑ __________ .____.____.____.____.____.____.____

3/29/2000

AVAILABILITY BY CENTURY:
This chart identifies the dates or the span of time the document existed

SOURCE DOCUMENTS:
These are original papers that identify individuals at the time of an event.

Robert R Langman, Ph D
84 West 7500 South
Midvale, Utah 84047
(801)568-0154

UNITED STATES
Research Checklist
Family Name____________________
Locality____________________

LOCATION:
The location is where source documents can be found

SOURCE DOCUMENTS FOR RESEARCH

HOME

- ☐ Albums, Photographs
- ☐ Diaries, Journals
- ☐ Family Bible and Letters
- ☐ Internet
- ☐ Interviews
- ☐ Traditions

TOWN RECORDS

- ☐ Cemetery Records
- ☐ City or County Records
- ☐ Funeral Home Records
- ☐ Histories
- ☐ Newspaper Files
- ☐ Public School Records

COUNTY RECORDS

- ☐ Administration of Estates
- ☐ Civil & Criminal Court Records
- ☐ County Historical Society
- ☐ Deeds & Mortgages
- ☐ Militia Records
- ☐ Naturalization Tax and Voter's Lists
- ☐ Probate, Wills, Guardianships
- ☐ Sheriff's Sales
- ☐ Tax and Voter's Lists
- ☐ Vital Records: Birth/Marriage/Death

STATE RECORDS

- ☐ Accounts & Journals
- ☐ Homestead & Donation Land Claims
- ☐ Land Grants
- ☐ State Archives
- ☐ State Census
- ☐ State Historical Society
- ☐ Supreme & Appellate Court Records
- ☐ Vital Records

NATIONAL RECORDS

- ☐ Bounty Land Records
- ☐ Census (1790-1920)
- ☐ Circuit Court of Appeals
- ☐ District & Supreme Court Records
- ☐ Immigration Records
- ☐ Military Land Grants & Military Records
- ☐ Mortality Schedules - Census years
- ☐ National Archives
- ☐ National Historical Society
- ☐ Passenger Lists
- ☐ Pay Vouchers and Pension Records
- ☐ Public and Private Land Claims
- ☐ Vital Registration

LIBRARIES

- ☐ Biographical Compendia
- ☐ C D Pro-Phone
- ☐ Cemetery Records
- ☐ Church Records & Histories
- ☐ D A R Lineage Books
- ☐ D A R Patriot Index
- ☐ Directories to funeral homes&cemeteries
- ☐ Genealogies
- ☐ Interlibrary Loan
- ☐ Newspapers on Microfilm
- ☐ Obituary Collections and Indexes
- ☐ Printed and Manuscript Histories

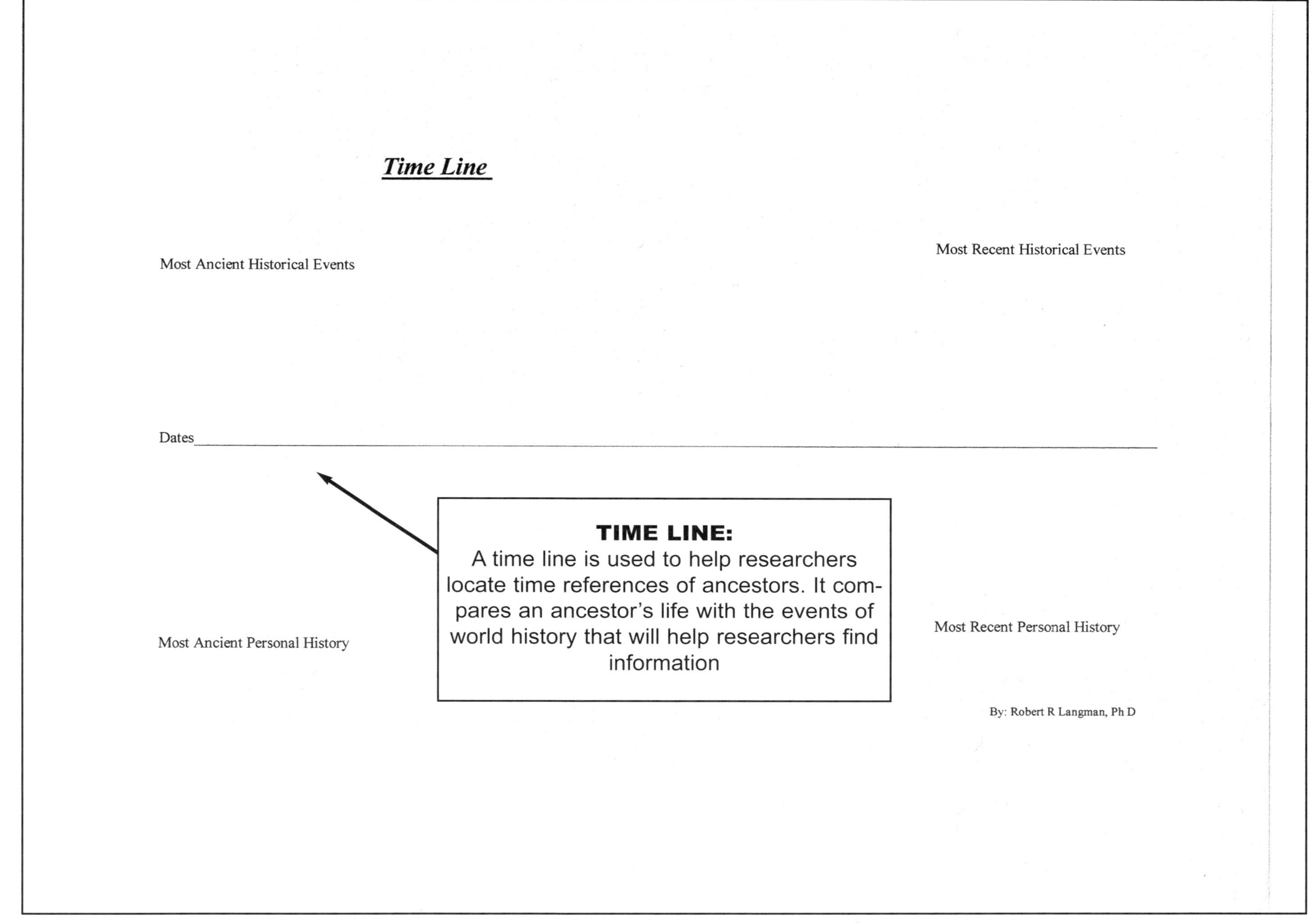

Time Line

Most Ancient Historical Events

Most Recent Historical Events

Dates____

TIME LINE:
A time line is used to help researchers locate time references of ancestors. It compares an ancestor's life with the events of world history that will help researchers find information

Most Ancient Personal History

Most Recent Personal History

By: Robert R Langman, Ph D

RESEARCH LOG

By: Jimmy B Parker

Ancestor's Name ______________________

Date ________

Collection or Call Number	**Description of Source** (Country, Book or Film, Author, Title, Type of Document)	Date Searched	Results

RESEARCH LOG:
A research log is used to write down needed information for future reference.

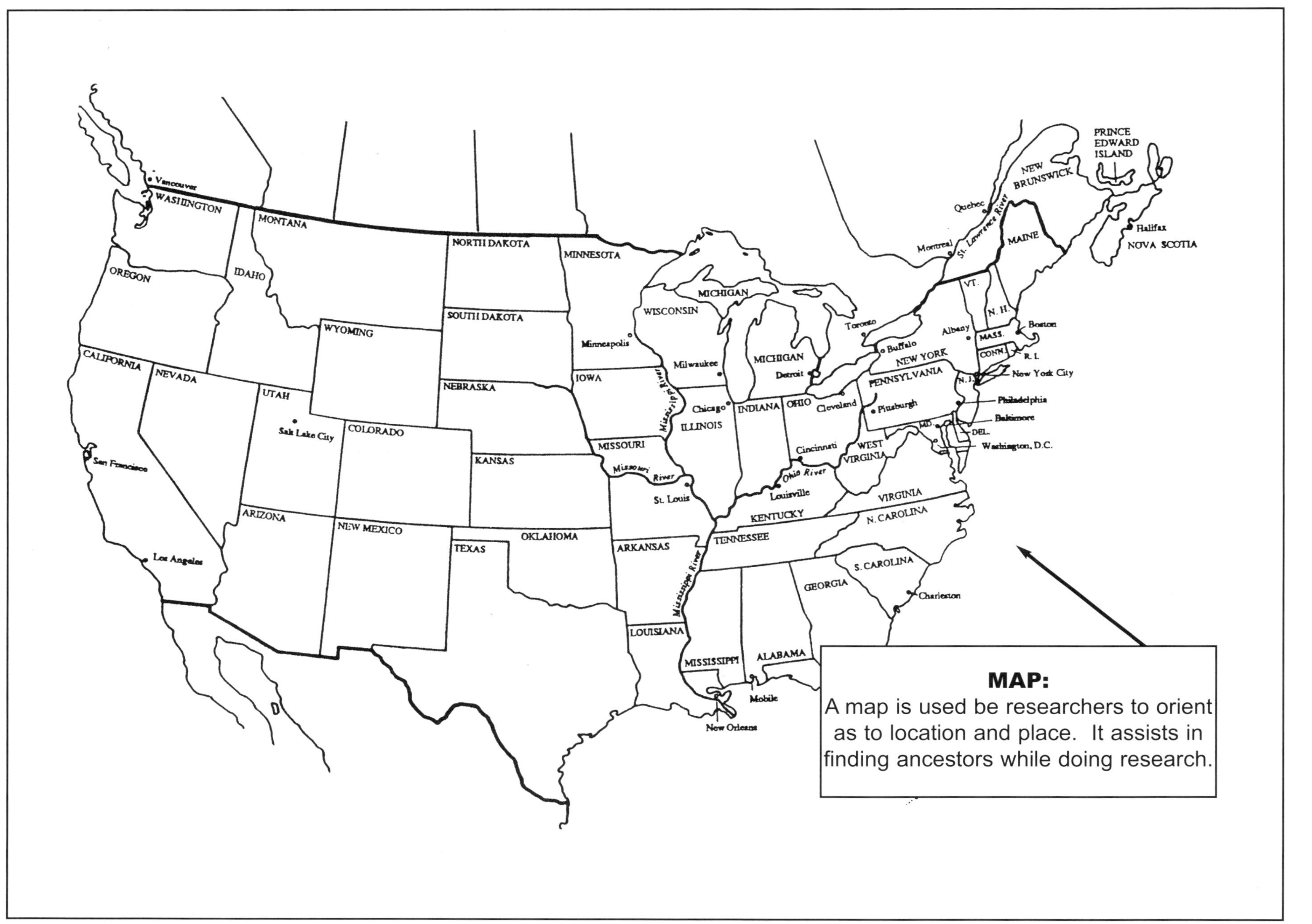
PRINCE EDWARD ISLAND
NEW BRUNSWICK
NOVA SCOTIA
Halifax
Quebec
Montreal
St. Lawrence River
MAINE
VT.
N. H.
MASS.
Boston
CONN.
R. I.
New York City
Albany
NEW YORK
Buffalo
Toronto
PENNSYLVANIA
Pittsburgh
N. J.
Philadelphia
Baltimore
DEL.
MD.
Washington, D.C.
WEST VIRGINIA
VIRGINIA
N. CAROLINA
S. CAROLINA
Charleston
GEORGIA
ALABAMA
Mobile
MISSISSIPPI
New Orleans
LOUISIANA
TENNESSEE
KENTUCKY
Louisville
Ohio River
Cincinnati
OHIO
Cleveland
MICHIGAN
Detroit
INDIANA
ILLINOIS
Chicago
Milwaukee
WISCONSIN
MICHIGAN
Mississippi River
St. Louis
Missouri River
MISSOURI
ARKANSAS
IOWA
MINNESOTA
Minneapolis
NORTH DAKOTA
SOUTH DAKOTA
NEBRASKA
KANSAS
OKLAHOMA
TEXAS
NEW MEXICO
COLORADO
WYOMING
MONTANA
IDAHO
UTAH
Salt Lake City
ARIZONA
NEVADA
CALIFORNIA
San Francisco
Los Angeles
OREGON
WASHINGTON
Vancouver
MAP:
A map is used be researchers to orient as to location and place. It assists in finding ancestors while doing research.

Cut-out examples

Geneology Research

To Do List

*Name to research*__________________________________

*Date Started*______________________

1.

2.

3.

4.

5.

6.

7.

8.

9.

10.

11.

12.

13.

14.

15.

List of Searches

Date: ______________________

Surname of Interest ____

Locality ____

Research Facility ____

Call No.	Description of Source	. . . Date Searched	Extract Number

Robert R Langman, Ph D
84 West 7500 South
Midvale, Utah 84047
(801) 568-0154

UNITED STATES AND CANADA

Research Checklist

Family Name____

Locality____

RESEARCH AND BACKGROUND INFORMATION
In Family History Library at Salt Lake City, Utah

- ❑ Ancestral File
- ❑ Family Group Records Collection (Archive)
- ❑ Family Group Records Collection (Patron)
- ☐ Family Registry
- ☐ International Genealogical Index
- ☐ Temple Records Index Bureau
- ☐ Family Histories

- ❑ Atlases, maps
- ❑ Biographies
- ❑ Catalogs, indexes and bibliographies
- ❑ Gazetteers
- ❑ Local histories
- ❑ Periodicals
- ❑ Periodical indexes

SOURCE DOCUMENTS FOR RESEARCH

AVAILABILITY BY CENTURY
14th 15th 16th 17th 18th 19th 20th

❑ State censuses____(various)____________________._____._____._____._____._XXX.XXXX.XXXX

❑ Wills or administrations____________________._____._____._____.___X.XXXX.XXXX.XXXX

❑ Passenger indexes____________________._____._____._____.___X._XXX.XXXX.XXXX

❑ Passenger lists____________________._____._____._X__.___X._XXX.XXXX.XXXX

❑ Federal censuses and indexes____________________._____._____._____.___X.XXXX.XXXX.X___

❑ Deeds, mortgages____________________._____._____._____.___X.XXXX.XXXX.XXXX

❑ Military pensions____________________._____._____._____.XXXX.XXXX.XXXX.XXXX

❑ Military service files____________________._____._____._____.XXXX.XXXX.XXXX.XXXX

❑ Naturalization declarations (1st papers) ____________________._____._____._X__._XXX.XXXX.XXXX.XXXX

❑ Naturalization petitions (2nd papers)____________________._____._____._X__._XXX.XXXX.XXXX.XXXX

❑ Birth____________________._____.___X.XXXX.XXXX.XXXX.XXXX.XXXX

❑ Civil Marriage____________________._____.___X.XXXX.XXXX.XXXX.XXXX.XXXX

❑ Death____________________._____.___X.XXXX.XXXX.XXXX.XXXX.XXXX

❑ Church marriage, burial____________________._____.___X.XXXX.XXXX.XXXX.XXXX.XXXX

❑ Baptism____________________._____._XXX.XXXX.XXXX.XXXX.XXXX.XXXX

❑ Tombstone, sexton record____________________._____._XXX.XXXX.XXXX.XXXX.XXXX.XXXX

❑ ____________________._____._____._____._____._____._____

3/29/2000

Time Line

Most Ancient Historical Events

Most Recent Historical Events

Dates____

Most Ancient Personal History

Most Recent Personal History

By: Robert R Langman, Ph D